Globalization and Sustainable Tourism Development

Globalization and Sustainable Tourism Development

By

Dr. M. Lakshmi Narasaiah
M.A., Ph.D.

Professor & Head
Department of Economics
Sri Krishnadevaraya University Post-graduate Centre
Kurnool–518 002
Andhra Pradesh (India)

DPH

DISCOVERY PUBLISHING HOUSE
NEW DELHI

First Published–2004
Reprint : 2012

ISBN: 81-7141-851-1

Published by:
DISCOVERY PUBLISHING HOUSE
4831/24, Prahlad Street, Ansari Road, Darya Ganj
New Delhi–110 002 (India)
Phone: 23279245, • Fax: 91-11-23253475
e-mail: dphtemp@indiatimes.com

Printed At :- Dynamic Printers,Delhi

Preface

Tourism has grown into one of the world's major industries and has thus also become an increasingly important, if complex, issue for environmental policy. Unless it is developed in a sustainable manner, we will be unable to achieve key objectives of global environmental policy such as the preservation of biological diversity, the prevention of climate change or the conservation of natural resources.

Tourism itself depends a lot on the existence of unspoilt nature and landscapes, as well as a healthy environment. If nature is plundered, landscapes are destroyed or water, energy and soil resources are over-exploited, the economic basis of tourism is also undermined. The needs of tourism do therefore overlap with those of environmental protection and nature conservation.

On the one hand, for instance, tourists are becoming increasingly environmentally conscious and are looking to get back to nature and enjoy unspoilt environments when on holiday. On the other hand, however, the number of international tourists is growing constantly. The proportion of long-haul journeys is also increasing steadily, especially in the industrialised nations, where travel s now taken for granted as part of people's lifestyles and has become an important factor in social status. The many different types of travel and holidays are covering more and more countries and regions and, as a result, increasing numbers of previously unspoilt natural environments are being opened up to tourism. This applies equally to coastlines, small islands, coral reefs, rock formations and mountain regions.

There is growing recognition of the need for tourism to develop in a sustainable and environmentally friendly manner. Many countries have, for instance, introduced regulations which require environmental impact surveys to be carried out at least for larger tourist developments. Since the Rio Summit in 1992, there have also been more initiatives in support of sustainable tourism at international level.

- Sustainable tourism allows for the rational use of biological diversity and can contribute to the preservation of that diversity.
- The development of tourism must be controlled and carefully managed so that it remains sustainable.
- Particular attention must be paid to tourism in ecologically and culturally sensitive areas, where mass tourism should be avoided.
- All parties concerned, including in particular the private sector, have a part to play in bringing about the sustainable development of tourism, and voluntary initiatives (codes of conduct, quality labels) should be encouraged.
- Particular importance should be attached to the local level, which is not only responsible for the sustainable development of tourism but should also derive particular benefit from tourism.

It will mark the successful beginning of internationally coordinated efforts to make tourism environmentally and socially sustainable so that many generations to come can continue to experience and enjoy the beauty of nature on our planet.

Dr. M. Lakshmi Narasaiah

Contents

1

Democracy and the Market Economy

Today the idea of democracy is triumphant; the model is in principle embraced in most countries the world over. You may say that the very word democracy has been hailed and misused earlier in history. The most repressing and totalitarian regimes have tried to mask themselves as "real" or "peoples" democracies. What has happened, however, is a historical demasking of these false pretences.

What exactly do we mean by democracy? There is now a general agreement that democracy cannot be defined by purpose or policy or levels of mass mobilisation. It must be defined as a political system where different parties or individuals compete for power through regular free elections where all adult citizens have a vote. Moreover, a democracy must uphold certain basic human rights and well-defined freedoms which make the political process possible, and respect the opinion and integrity of the individual. No other definitions hold, and we should be careful when we talk about "real" democracy versus "formal" democracy. A society which in real life upholds the constitutional or formal democratic principles and which in practice applies the rights these principles imply, is by definition a democracy. A society with a beautiful-sounding constitution but where none or few of these rights are respected is certainly not a democracy.

Democratic Government no Guarantee for Equality

It is important to understand that democratic government does not necessarily mean good government in the sense that those in power make wise or well-considered decisions. Nor does it mean that conflicts inherent in the society are reduced to a minimum. Demands for democracy, social justice and a better life have historically gone hand in hand, but this does not mean that the establishment of a democratic system actually does lead to an improvement in social conditions or equality. It is also quite clear that some societies have a sort of outer shell of democracy but in reality, exclude large groups of people from having any political influence whatsoever. The actual differences in living conditions are so enormous and so entrenched that these people have no confidence at all in the political system even if it is democratic according to the definition. In these cases—for example in some Latin American countries—one can talk of a "masked hegemony with competing elites" where the outcome of struggles for power has little relevance for the masses. It is a sort of social and political half-authoritarian system—but disguised as a democracy-where the military often have a significant influence.

In the rhetoric of the day the terms market economy and democracy are used as if they were synonymous or at least naturally emerging at the same time. But this is wrong—or at-least misleading. When the market economy or capitalism finally established itself in the 1800s and came to characterize modern industrial civilisation, democracy was at best in its infancy. In fact one could argue that democracy grew out of the contradictions and social dynamism inherent in the market economy of the capitalistic system. In this century we have a long list of terrifying and repressive regimes which have nevertheless upheld the virtues of a market economy. That some of these regimes have for ideological and security reason been hailed as bastions against communism, and also dignified members of the so-called free world does not transform them into democracies. In this company it is perhaps unnecessary to remind ourselves that the colonial system was assuredly not democratic, but was certainly based on capitalistic or market economic principles. It is the sad but irrefutable historical coupling between Western democracy, colonialism, and the plundering of resources in the name of the market economy which for understandable reasons meant that many of the leaders of national liberation movements looked for other models for the development of their young nations. In this connection it can be worth remembering what Nelson Mandela said soon after his release from 26 years of prison in the market economic but racist state of South Africa. "When we in ANC during 40 years struggled for democracy we were put in prison by the same people who are now telling us how we should behave to promote the democracy we have been rejected by all these years".

While we can see that a market economy does not automatically lead to democracy, a functioning democracy—as we have defined it—does seem to require some form of free economic system.

Democracy and Economic Freedom

Theoretically, it is conceivable that a political democracy could be combined with an economy totally controlled by the government—but experience has shown this to be very difficult. One could even argue that it is by definition impossible since democracy implies a certain freedom of economic choice and independent economic actors. A functioning democratic system presupposes what is now often referred to as a civil—society-in practice, independent institutions, companies, organisations, the media etc., regulated by law but not subject to or controlled by those in power.

We must also see clearly that there are no unambiguous relations between economic growth, development and democracy. Democratic governments are neither very successful when it comes to structural reforms which may be to the disadvantage of important interests in the society, nor when it comes to welfare. The developing countries which have achieved the greatest success economically and socially over the last 20 years are the East Asian countries—which all have had various kinds of more are less authoritarian systems.

However, that does not mean that you can use these countries as models for the rest of the world. There is no globally valid link between an authoritarian form of regime and economic development, not even when development is defined only in terms of autocentric growth. Many social scientists—have tried to find some systematic connection between what we call development or modernisation on the one hand, and the political system on the other—but all have failed.

It is also obvious that one of several pre-requisites for economic growth and development is legitimate and reasonably well functioning government and governance. If the free market is to be a motor for development and improved welfare, and not just a meeting place for robber barons, the mafia and speculators, you must have a regulating and supportive state. If economic history teaches us anything, it is just this. Consider the astounding development in Germany after the war, or in Japan and the other East Asian countries some years later. There are many differences, but what they have in common is a well-functioning government apparatus with a long tradition.

Today we find ourselves in a historical situation where a large number of countries in the former communist states of Europe, in Africa, Asia and Latin America are at one and the same time trying to establish a new democratic system and new economic mechanisms. The situation is unique, and the intrinsic problems are unprecedented. Democracy as an idea has triumphed but in its practice it is in profound trouble. It is no exaggeration to talk of the crisis of democracy.

The former communist countries are certainly in crisis. As a by-product of the past regimes, there is an intensive suspicion of the political institutions, of the state and the parties—and in this way also the legitimacy of democracy and the ability of the politicians to deal with the fundamental problems of society has been undermined. The lack of a democratic tradition is not overcome from one day to the next.

Many of the developing countries have similar difficulties the introduction of a multiparty system does not in itself mean that one can manage the conflicts and social problems in a democratic way.

Countries in Transition

Both in the East and the South countries are trying, at one and the same time, to change the political and economic system. When the whole society is convulsed by economic changes, and where peoples' living conditions fundamentally change, it is not easy to develop and maintain a political system based on compromise and respect, including respect for minorities.

As in previous history the deep crises of legitimacy and general frustration feed national and ethnical conflicts. These conflicts establish themselves in societies where the authoritarian system, economic crises and the break down of traditional values rob people of any kind of kinship other than ethnical.

We cannot avoid seeing disturbing signs of this crisis of democracy also in the so-called "established democracies" of the rich countries.

It is obvious that the state of democracy varies from country to country, as do the reasons for a feeling of dejection. But there are some similarities too.

The continuing and noticeable internationalisation limits the national freedom of political choice, available alternatives, and makes it more difficult for people to see the connection between "politics" and their actual living conditions. The governments are restrained by international economic events. The reaction of the stock exchange may be more important than that of the voters. The election results influence the stock exchange prices—but is it perhaps not also so that the stock exchanges, indirectly, also influence the election results? People feel themselves to be the victims of major economic changes, but no one seems to be responsible and they themselves feel they have little chance of influencing the outcome. The absence of clearly identifiable alternatives between the larger political parties provides between the larger political parties provides opportunities for the populists and the extremists.

There is indeed reason to reflect on the lessons of the history of our turbulent and cruel century.

Priority for Growth

There is today much concern about the lack of resources for such urgent needs as the reconstruction of the East, a concerted attack on poverty and human development in the poorest countries, and environmental investments of all kinds. If the growth of world output returns to the levels of the 1980s, total output would grow by about one trillion dollars a year. There is, in fact, no other way to resolve the economic and political crises multiplying in the world community than to give priority to the restoration of growth.

We are certainly not at the end of history as someone has argued. We are rather at a dramatic turning point, a moment of many possibilities and many dangers. What we do now, for a few years ahead, may direct the future for several decades—like the dramatic and fateful years immediately after the second world war. All nations, all governments, have a responsibility. The rich world has a special responsibility, not just moral because of its enormous economic and political power.

2

The Challenges of Globalization

Globalization gives rise in some quarters to fears that can lead to suspicion, protectionism, and policies that are ultimately self-destructive. Such fears cannot be allowed to frustrate the great potential of a world in which countries drawing closer together. We believe that countries can face the challenges of globalization positively, demanding as those challenges may be.

All countries can benefit from full participation in the world's markets, including its financial markets. Protectionist pressures must be resisted and reversed, and the principles of openess and mulilaterism promoted by the World Trade Organisation, the IMF, and the World Bank must be honoured. And financial market integration should be seen as a positive force: it offers access to global financial intermediation and a stimulus for more competitive and efficient domestic financial sectors: and it promotes efficiency and growth worldwide.

How encouraging it is, therefore, to see that so many developing countries in transition have been freeing up their trade and exchange systems within the framework of our structural adjustment programs.

No country can afford to forgo the benefits of integration into global market: the alternative is marginalization and stagnation. But all countries must take the steps to minimize the associated risks. More than ever before, countries need tightly disciplined macro economic policies to maintain a stable environment for investors, whether domestic or foreign. And while foreign capital can be a useful—and sometimes vital complement to domestic saving, it is not a substitute for it: domestic saving remains the key to investment and sustainable growth. It is also clear that strong financial institutions are essential to avoid market disturbances at home and to secure an effective defense against external pressures. Competitive banking and financial systems that are sound, well regulated, and properly supervised are indispensable for countries to be able to expose their economies safely to the pressures that can arise in global markets.

The challenges to globalization therefore add to the need for the developing and transition countries to press ahead with their adjustment and reform efforts. For many, this means creating conditions to attract foreign, financing and use it effectively. But a growing number of countries, have been facing a different problem: how to cope with large-scale capital inflows. Such inflows, especially when they are easily reversible, provide no grounds for relaxation of adjustment and reform.

They should not be used to finance domestic consumption. In many cases, they call foe stronger fiscal discipline; and in some cases, exchange rates should be allowed to take part of the strain. Many developing countries and countries in transition also, of course, need to do more to deepen and widen the role of market forces and to foster more competitive market environments, in order to promote transparent and efficient mechanisms for resource allocation.

Is globalization any less demanding for the industrial countries? Not at all! It adds to the urgency of the task of taking full advantage of the current expansion to tackle the deep-rooted problems that are limiting the pace, the quality, and perhaps, the sustainability of their growth.

All has to applaud the increased efforts and commitments to reduce fiscal deficits, but in most cases underlying imbalances remain large and the pace of consolidation too slow. More must be done not only to redress present imbalances but also to meet the growing demands of the future.

Another deep-rooted problem-structural unemployment—must also be tackled sooner, rather than later. Budget laxity and high unemployment tend to feed on each other. While cyclical conditions provide the opportunity, governments must not flinch from the task of improving the functioning of labor markets. How? It is not an easy task: by reforming regulations and policies that impede employment creation and job search.

Monetary stability, macroeconomic discipline, sound financial systems, and efficiently working market mechanisms are essential for all countries that embrace globalization. But they are not sufficient for any. To fight the fears that globalization sometimes inspires, countries need policies that promote not just economic efficiency, financial stability, and growth but also equity and high-quality growth. In too many countries, the quality of growth suffers from widening distributional inequalities related partly to high unemployment but also stagnating wages of unskilled workers. And too many countries continue to suffer from poor governance, corruption and increasing crime.

Of course, economic policy can provide only part of what is needed to rid the world of these blights. But it is a vital part. To promote equity, efficiency, and sustainable growth, governments carry an inescapable responsibility for investment in human capital—through education, health care, and well-targeted social safety nets—and also for establishing and maintaining honest and effective systems of public administration, law, order and justice. If these essential services are to be affordable, there is certainly no room for unproductive expenditures—military or otherwise—and wasteful subsidies: they must bear the brunt of fiscal consolidation. So globalization demands a lot from governments if it is to deliver its promise of stronger and high-quality growth.

3

Globalization: A Moral Imperative

Globalization has become today's buzzword. It has also become a battle ground for two radically opposed groups. There are the anti-globalists, who fear globalization and stress only its downside, seeking therefore powerful interventions aimed at taming, if not (unwittingly) crippling it. Then there are the "globalists" (a class to which I belong) who celebrate globalization instead, emphasize its upside, while seeking only to ensure that its few rough edges be handled through appropriate policies that serve to make globalization yet more attractive.

Many anti-globalists consider the central problem of globalization to be its amorality, or even its immorality. But these critics have too blanket an approach to globalization. The word covers a variety of phenomena that characterize an integrating world economy: trade, short-term capital flows, direct foreign investment, immigration, cultural convergence et al. The sins of one of the above cannot be visit upon the virtues of another. Some are benign even when largely unregulated whereas others can be fatal if left wholly to the marketplace.

In particular, the freeing of trade is largely benign: if I exchange some of my toothpaste for some of your toothbrushes, we will both be better off than if we did not trade at all. It would require a wild imagination, and a deranged mind, to think that such freeing of trade leads to debilitating economic crises. Equally, it is illogical to believe, as non-economists who fear globalization do, that freeing of trade is bad because the freeing of short-term capital flows led to a debilitating financial and economic crises and could do so again. In fact, while there are some obvious simulates between free trade and free capital flows—e.g. that segmentation of markets creates efficiency losses—the economic and political dissimilarities are even more compelling and policymakers cannot ignore them.

Anti-globalist critics are in fact often reacting viscerally to a much larger issue: the victory of capitalism over its arch rival, communism. For campus idealists who have always looked for alternatives to what they conventionally consider to be the greed and lack of social conscience that characterize capitalism, the situation is psychologically intolerable. Some have turned to street theatre, nihilism and the antiintellectualism that has been manifest in the last few years. The more sophisticated have succumbed to a stereotypical representation of corporation as the evil forces of capitalism that have captured the state, democratic institutions, and even international bodies such as the World Trade Organization.

What these critics often forget is that certain economic freedoms are basic to prosperity and social well-being under any conditions, and are thus of the highest moral value. Property rights and markets, for instance, provide incentives to produce and allocate resources efficiently, and can in turn strengthen democracy by allowing a means of sustenance out side pervasive government structures. The quality and breadth of democracy can then be enlarged as excluded groups, such as women and the poor, are pulled into literacy, gainful employment and better health through higher public spending or the spread of economic incentives.

Critics nevertheless go on to maintain that the global spread of free markets and free trade is responsible for continuing poverty in poor countries, and for alleged growth in inequality between and within countries. Labour unions in the rich countries also fear that trade in cheap labour-using goods from poor countries.

But I do not think these concerns are wellfounded. In India which has almost a quarter of the world's poor, there is good evidence that autarchic and anti-market policies produced abysmally low growth rates at 3.5 percent annually over a quarter of a century, with a correspondingly negligible impact on poverty has declined. Higher growth rates in turn depend on several factors; but openness to trade and direct investment and a skilful use of markets are definitely and important contributory factor.

As for inequality among nations, it is precisely those countries that embraced integration into the world economy, i.e. the Far Eastern Four and then the ASEAN countries, which raced ahead with dramatic growth rates whereas several countries of Africa, Latin America and Asia that looked inwards failed to deliver growth and also made little dent on poverty.

The evidence on trade and investment impoverishing our workers is also flawed. My own research suggests that the downward pressure on workers' wages due to technical change has been dampened, not magnified, by trade with the poor countries. Research also shows that big corporations use abroad technologies similar to those at home, instead of exploiting lower standards or forcing them yet lower through their financial clout.

One result of these mistaken arguments against globalization has been an insistent clamour for certain environmental and labour standard to be linked to rules on international trade. But by seeking to create new obstacles to free trade, you undermine the freeing of trade, while mixing up trade with a moral agenda undermines that very moral agenda. It gives other countries the definite impression that you are using ethical rhetoric to mask protectionist self-interest.

The notion that global free trade and investment are responsible for poverty, inequality, lowering of standards and harming social progress is little short of astonishing. Yet national politicians and international bureaucrats give it who think that going along is way of getting along. In denying the virtues of globalization, they actually harm the very causes they profess to embrace.

4

The Truth About Global Competition—The Economic Myths behind Globalization

Local communities everywhere are on the front lines of what might well be characterized as World War III. It is not the nuclear confrontation between East and West—between the Soviet Union and the United States—that we once feared. It is a very different kind of conflict. There is no clash of competing military forces and the struggle is not defined by national borders. But it does involve an often violent struggle for control of physical resources and territory that is destroying lives and communities at every hand. It is a struggle between the forces and institutions of economic globalization and the communities that are trying to reclaim control of their economic lives. It is a conflict between competing goals—economic growth to maximize profits for absentee owners versus creating healthy communities that are good placed for people to live. It is a competition for the control of markets and resources between global corporations and financial markets on the one hand and locally owned businesses serving local markets on the other.

Two things of fundamental importance to each and every one of us are now very much at stake.

- Will people and communities control their local resources and economies and be able to set their own goals and priorities based on their own values and aspiration? Or will these decisions be left to global financial markets and corporations that are blind to all values save one—instant financial returns?

- Will the life sustaining resources produced by the regenerative capacities of our planet's ecosystems be equitably shared to provide for the material needs of all of us who inhabit this bountiful planet, as well as for our children and their children unto the seventh generation and beyond? Or will we allow a global economic system that is now functioning on auto-pilot beyond conscious human control to consume and destroy the ecosystem and our social fabric in its insatiable quest for money?

Economists, politicians, cooperate spokespersons and the media have for years been touting the benefits of the global economy. They have called on us to support trade agreements such as the North American Free Trade Agreement (NAFTA) and the World Trade Organization (WTO) to remove the constraints of economic borders and open to everyone the opportunities of growth and prosperity in the global economy. They have promised rich rewards for those workers and communities that become successful global competitors.

Many of the most ardent boosters of economic globalization met earlier in the year at the annual meeting of the World Economic Forum. This Forum has for years brought together top industrialists and political figures from around the world to advance the proposition that removing tariffs and other restrictions on the free international flow of trade and money is a key to creating new economic opportunity and prosperity. It thus cause quite a stir when the Forum publicly announced that economic globalization is producing disastrious consequences that threaten the political stability of the Western democracies. Their warning bears close examination for being one of the most honest and accurate assessments of the consequences of economic globalization yet produced by leading advocates of that process. The observation is that:

- Economic globalization is causing severe economic dislocation and social instability.
- The technological changes of the past few years have eliminated more jobs than they have created.
- The global competition "that is part and parcel of globalization leads to winner-take-all situations; those who come out on top win big, and the losers lose even bigger."
- Higher profits no longer mean more job security and better wages. "Globalization tends to delink the fate of the corporation from the fate of its employees."
- Unless serious corrective action is taken soon, the backlash could destabilize the Western democracies.

We don't have to go far to find examples of what they are talking about the why people are getting a bit upset as they wake up to the realities of who is winning in the ruthless competition of the global economy. The disparities between the winners and losers in the global competition are becoming more obscene with each passing day.

We are coming to realize that the extravagant promises of the advocates of the global economy are based on a number of myths that have become so deeply embedded in Western industrial culture that we have grown to accept them without examination.

- The myth that growth in *GNP* is a valid measure of human well-being and progress.
- The myth that free unregulated markets efficiently allocate a society's resources.
- The myth that growth in trade benefits ordinary people.
- The myth that global corporations are benevolent institutions that if freed from governmental interference will provide a clean environment for all and good jobs for the poor.

- The myth that absentee investors create local prosperity.

The Growth Myth

Our measures of growth are deeply flawed in that they are purely measures of activity in the monetized economy. Expanded use of cigarettes and alcohol increases economic output both as a direct consequence of their consumption and because of the related increase in health care needs. The need to clean up oil spills generates economic activity. Gun sales to minors generate economic activity. A divorce generates both lawyers fees and the need to buy or rent and outfit a new home increasing real estate brokerage fees and retail sales. It is now well documented that in number of other countries the quality of living of ordinary people has been declining as aggregate economic output increases.

The growth myth has another serious flaw. Since 1950, the world's economic output has increased 5 to 7 times. That growth has already increased the human burden on the planet's regenerative systems—its soils, air, water, fisheries, and forestry systems—beyond what the planet can sustain. Continuing to press for economic growth beyond the planet's sustainable limits does two things. It accelerates the rate of breakdown of the earth's regenerative systems—as we see so dramatically demonstrated in the case of many ocean fisheries, and it intensifies the competition between rich and poor for the resource base that remains.

This is vividly illustrated by many of the development projects in India many funded with loans from the World Bank and other multilateral development banks—that displace the poor so that the lands and waters on which they depend for their livelihood can be converted to uses that generate higher economic returns—meaning converted to use by people who can pay more than those who are displaced.

The Myth of Free Unregulated Markets

It is almost inherent in the nature of markets that their efficient function depends on the presence of a strong government to set a framework of rules for their operation. We know that free markets create monopolies, which government must break up to maintain the conditions of competition on which market function depends.

We also know that markets only allocate efficiently when prices reflect the full and true costs of production. Yet in the absence of governmental regulation, market incentives persistently push firms to cut corners on safety, pay workers less than a living wages, and dump untreated toxic discharges into a convenient river. In our present competitive context if management does not take such measures, they are likely to be replaced by the owners or bought out by someone with less scruples who will.

The Myth of Free Trade

Many so-called trade agreements, such as the North American Free Trade Agreement (NAFTA) and the World Trade Organization (WTO) are not really trade agreements at all. They are economic integration agreements intended to guarantee the rights of global corporations to move both goods and investments where ever they wish—free from public interference and accountability. WTO is best described as a bill of rights for global corporations.

The Myth that Economic Globalization is Inevitable

Many of the people who claim globalization is a consequence of inevitable historical forces are paid to promote that message by the same global corporations that have invested millions of dollars in advancing the globalization policy agenda.

The Myth that Corporations are Benevolent Institutions

The corporation is an institutional invention specifically and internationally created to concentrate control over economic resources while shielding those who hold the resulting power from liability for the consequences of its use. The more national economies become integrated into a seamless global economy, the further corporate power extends beyond the reach of any state and the less accountable it becomes to any human interest or institution other than a global financial system that is now best described as a gigantic legal gambling casino.

All over the world people are indeed waking up to the truth about economic globalization and are taking steps to reclaim and rebuild their local economies. Such communities face basic choices as to how they will divide their efforts between competing for a share of the declining pool of good jobs that global corporations offer and working to create locally owned enterprises that sustainably harvest and process local resources to produce the jobs and the goods and services that local people need to live healthy, happy, and fulfilling lives in balance with the environment.

Our experience with the real consequences of economic globalization is pointing to many important lessons. One such lesson is that economies should be local, rooting power in the people and communities who realize their well-being depends on the health and vitality of their local ecosystem. If it is protectionist to favor local firms and workers who pay local taxes, live by local rules, respect and nurture the local ecosystems, compete fairly in local markets, and contribute to community life—then let us all proudly proclaim ourselves to be protectionist.

Such choices are not isolationist. To the contrary, they create a foundation for creative cooperation with our neighbours—whether they be in the United States or in other countries—to share experience, ideas, and technology—and to join in international solidarity in rewriting the rules of the global economy to favour local over global businesses, and to encourage cooperative relations among people and communities. It is our consciousness—our ways of thinking and our sense of membership in a larger community—not our economies—that should be global.

Millions of people are also making an important discovery—that life of is about living—not consuming. A life of material sufficiency can be filled with social, cultural, intellectual, and spiritual abundance that place no burden on the planet.

It is time to assume responsibility for creating a new human future of just and sustainable communities freed from the myth that greed, competition, and mind-less consumption are paths to individual and collective fulfilment. It will take millions of people around the world-linked together into a powerful political coalition aimed at radical political and economic—reform to win the war that global capital is waging against us.

5

The Nation State and Globalisation

The world has changed dramatically. Some of the changes are as yet only dimly understood. We are all going to be confronted with many challenges to the whole concept of government and to the role of the nation state as we move into the next century.

There are two principal aspects to these changes. Globalisation of the world economies is sharply limiting the independence of action of the nation state. In addition, we are only just beginning to understand what the existence of one superpower, supreme militarily, financially, means to the evolution of world diplomacy and world politics.

These remarks are directed to the first aspect. Governments are now losing influence. Private enterprise, capitalism, summarised as 'the market', is gaining power. Privatisation is a keyword. Across the political spectrum liberal, conservative and formerly socialist parties have all accepted the downsizing of government, the privatisation of many activities and the reduction of government debt. Governments in crisis in the developed or in the developing world have been left in no doubt about what they should do.

The International Monetary Fund and the World Bank have made it clear that assistance would not be available to countries in distress unless appropriate policies were put in place, and IMF prescriptions often involve substantial and detailed microeconomic reform within a country with considerable hardship for its people.

Meanwhile, competition for international capital has become much more severe. In the early independence years, Commonwealth countries believed they could write their own internal rules about the performance and behaviour of capital. Now those rules have to be rewritten to maximise international attraction. The relationship has to be competitive, the rule have to be friendly to capital. This is a totally different environment from the one in which most Commonwealth countries gained their independence in the immediate post war years.

The new global organisation of industry has significant consequences for social policy. Many governments would have conducted policies designed to see that workers gained a fair share of the returns of an enterprise. With the globalisation of industry, such policies are no longer possible. Governments now tend to argue for lower wages, for smaller workforces, to maximise the competitiveness of their particular country as a home for global corporations. This has consequences of enhancing the profit share as opposed to the wage share of particular enterprise.

One direct consequence of these changes is a significantly growing disparity in wealth between rich and poor in all countries worldwide. This may not matter so much if the poor were also becoming better off compared to their own earlier standards but in many cases this is not so. The idea of a living wage is no longer relevant. Workers in some countries are often paid a wage which could not support even the smallest of families. In this day, if that is what the market determines, then that is what must happen.

In today's world, governments must fashion their policies to meet the wishes of the international market place. There are fundamental differences from earlier times. The global organisation of industry in which national boundaries become irrelevant is certainly new. Some aspects of information technology can operate much faster and with more devastating effect than the old cable system of the last hundred years. This has led to an explosive growth in financial markets. The volume of money traded each day is huge (and) through modern communications, this finance has great mobility.

We all know enough of markets to know that they favour the powerful, the united and the strong and that markets can overwhelm and destroy smaller players. Sometimes smaller players are entire nations.

Those who suggest that the markets alone must be allowed to determine economic outcomes favour a world in which the large will do much better than the small. So far as countries are concerned, most Commonwealth countries are in the smaller category in a world in which large financial institutions and manufacturing corporations operating globally will dominate trade and commerce.

For most countries, banks and financial institutions, which are part of the culture of that country, will become a matter of the past. Banking services will be American, European, Japanese or perhaps Chinese. The consequences of this market dominance are clear. Corporations need a global spread and many national rules for the good order and conduct of business and commerce will no longer be relevant.

For the world as a whole, the most serious problem is volatility, possibly leading to systematic breakdown. Since the Asian economic problems of 1997, there has been a great deal of discussion about the present system and about changes that need to be made.

For a while it appeared that the United States really was going to move the reform process forward but now the tendency seem to be 'it's all right, we have escaped, leave well enough alone'... There is a need to reform the system, to establish much tougher international rules for prudential supervision and control. The IMF has demonstrated time and time again that it is not interested in avoiding crises, it is only interested in picking up the pieces after they have occurred. If this is its charter, it certainly needs reviewing. The IMF's present operations are inadequate.

Since governments have seemingly lost significant power to corporations and to financial markets and since they do operate within an increasingly globalised framework, individual governments are not capable of undertaking this task. The task is international and global. Whether it is a reformed IMF or a new institution is a matter for debate.

At their last meeting the Commonwealth Finance Ministers pointed to a number of changes, most of which are desirable, but there was no sense of great urgency, no sense of dynamism. They spoke of a need for new financial market architecture but nobody has tried to spell out what that means.

There are two specific tasks: how to preserve some form of equity and reasonable competition in a globalised market place and how to establish stability with the financial markets themselves.

The IMF's financial resources should be strengthened as a meas of averting crises through the provision of contingency funds. Immediate access to adequate funding can be essential for this purpose if crises are to be avoided. Finding a way to encourage the IMF to help avert crises instead of just reacting to crises after they have occurred is a most important requirement.

In any liquidity arrangement, assisting a country is distress, the IMF should take care not to absolve lenders of their responsibility. In some cases IMF bailouts have done more to help the lenders than the countries themselves. The lenders need to carry their own risk.

For poor countries, how to protect themselves and advance the welfare of their own people in an unpredictable world is a major challenge and very often a major problem. Apart from move to establish greater stability designed to avoid systematic breakdown within the world's financial system, there also need to be urgent moves to establish an international body to establish rules for fair trading in a globalised environment. Middle ranking and small countries would have most to gain from such an innovation.

6

Globalization and Knowledge Divide

Globalization looks very different when it is seen, not from the capitals of the West, but from the cities and villages of the South, where most of humanity lives. Four examples taken from India, illustrate how the paradoxical forces shaping globalization look when seen from the other side.

5 school children died in a remote village in India after drinking water and powdered milk mixed in a vat that had contained a powerful insecticide. Nobody could read the label of the vat and the children were poisoned. The insecticide in question has been banned in practically every industrialized nation; its sale continues only in places like my country.

Secondly, an important annual event recently took place in North India. Potato growers gather there to exchange the best seeds they have produced in the last year. It is an act of pride for communities to share with others seeds that will help improve the production of potatoes. A transnational corporation attended the festival and are now working to patent the genes of these traditional foodstuffs in order to sell them as profit.

India's macro-economic indicators are excellent. In the offices of investment bankers, you will be told that India is a great investment opportunity. The situation is not so rosy, however. Thirty percent of the population have been living below the poverty line for the last so many years. Ten per cent of the population are living below the critical poverty line: their income is insufficient to pay for event minimal nourishment. So much of the workforce is unemployed or under-employed.

A distinguished North American political scientist, Dr. Benjamin Barber, recently pointed out that in the United States democracy had degenerated into bringing one group of rascals in for four years, and then throwing them out and replacing them with another group of rascals for four years. From the perspective of the South, that looks very good! In a context where rascals manipulate elections and stay in power for fifteen or sixteen years, I would appreciate the chance to throw them out through peaceful elections every four years.

Thus, the complaints of the North are often the aspirations of the South. Progress in industrialized nations can be a threat to developing countries.

Ten years ago, in the euphoria of globalization and the expansion of services and finance that followed the fall of the Berlin Wall, I advanced the idea that we were entering a fractured global order. Globalization brings us into contact with one another, but it also strengthens profound divisions and fractures in terms of societies and income, and most importantly in our capacity to generate and utilize knowledge. Over the last ten years, the concentration of wealth and power has greatly increased both within and between societies.

There is a real risk of two civilizations emerging, with two ways of viewing and relating to the world: one based on the capacity to generate and utilize knowledge; the other passively receiving knowledge from abroad and deprived of the ability to modify it.

The world now faces the prospect of this Knowledge Divide becoming an unbridgeable abyss. We need the international community to return to the basic principles of international co-operation and introduce the idea that a minimum level of science and technological capability, including access to the Internet, is an absolute necessity for developing countries and should be the subject of international solidarity.

This can be achieved. However, contrary to the situation of 20 years ago, national governments are no longer the major players in the game of science and technology. Whether we like it or not, the private sector and the international community of scholars must be invited to the table with governments from the North and South to begin discussing an agenda for the mobilization of a science and technology for development. United Nations with a mandate for the development of the sciences, has a special role to play in the revitalization of international co-operation in this field.

7

Urbanization and Globalization

How we handle globalization will determine whether our cities and our civilization will be divided and violent or user-friendly and peaceful. We cannot get a clear picture of urban life in the 21st century, especially in the poor countries of the South, unless we take into account the phenomenon of globalization, which has already brought dramatic changes make their first appearance. So it is there too that the great upheavals of the next century will take place.

Globalization gives shape to the "Global Village". The "information era" that it ushers in compresses time and we are now living in a world speeded up as never before. Worldwide urbanization is proceeding at a similar rate and its pace in the poor countries of the South seems terrifying. By 2025, two-thirds of humanity will be living in cities and towns, where the best opportunities in life tend to be.

Globalization also accentuates a "new urban geography" in both North and South. Islands of rich consumers are springing up in cities amid an ocean of deprived people. More and more unemployed people, immigrants, minorities and the homeless, are pushed into cities by pressure from "market economies". As a result, all urban areas—not just those in the poor countries of the South—will have to deal with growing internal tensions. In New York, for example, the poorest 20 percent of the population earns 15 times less than the richest 20 per cent.

Cities have always had their smart neighbourhoods and their dangerous areas. But such social and geographical segregation has changed in pace and scale because of the growth in the urban population, the increase in "illegal" migrants and rising uncertainty.

In fact, we have entered a period of historical transition, where discontinuities prevail over adjustment. Radical changes in the nature of production and jobs and the incredible concentration of capital in the hands of the financial sector and speculators weigh much heavier in our lives these days than the state's efforts to adjust and improve the market economy. Segregation in cities has been given a new lease of life whose consequences we do not know. It has reached unprecedented dimensions because of the explosive growth of urban areas.

According to one scenario, things will go badly. The growing pace of globalization will increase uncertainty about the future. Fear and defence mechanisms will grow among people and institutions, fuelling intolerance, xenophobia and mistrust of everything new or foreign. Urban tensions will manifest themselves with increasing violence, and segregation will sharpen. Public areas will be abandoned and become dangerous no-man's-lands, the wretched abode of society's rejects. Cities will lose their original function of being a crossroads for meeting and exchange.

If globalization also continues to go hand in hand with deregulation of financial markets and an unchanged level of indebtedness of poor countries, the latter will not be able to maintain their urban infrastructures. And if on top of this there is corruption and lack of political will, challenges to the system will increase and violence will grow. Cash-strapped authorities will respond with undemocratic mafias which provide them with funds.

According to a second scenario, everything will be all right. In line with the principle that "everything the state does is public, but the state doesn't control everything that is public," a new social contract will be drawn up between the state, the market, the working population and civil society, including NGOs. Cities will develop a new quality of life by providing citizens with forum for exchange. Jobs will be created in the social sector, in the fields of the environment, education, research, culture and leisure, opening up possibilities for young people.

In the countries of the South, long-term development strategies will be drafted and urban planning practised, taking advantage of the opportunities provided by globalization but without falling into its traps. Town planning will become part of the political process, and the state will work with the private sector, monitored by institutions of civil society. Adequate housing will be built with the help of microcredit and controls on the price of building materials. Improved infrastructures will enable marginal areas to become part of the civilized part of the city. Democracy will come up with new ways of governing with the help of networks of involved citizens.

In a transitional scenario, action strategies should fall somewhere between these two extremes. They should include social goals so that in big urban areas a society emerges which is founded on participatory democracy and on "capitalism with a human face" or "market socialism".

But the outlook is less clear than ever. Let us hope the present transition will lead rapidly to a new revival of humanism, whose first signs we are already seeing. This would open up the road to a development which is fair, humane and peaceful.

8

Renewing the State

Many view globalization as a technology driven global order that has led to an intensification of interconnectedness among nations. This, however, is merely one fact of globalization, and does not presuppose the ideological homogenization or the rapid retrenchment of the welfare state that is currently underway.

The dispute over globalization is not about the intensification of global interconnectedness. Rather, it is over the vision of the global system that globalization projects. This vision entails a global economic system with identifiable rules of behaviour in trade, finance, taxation, investment policy, intellectual property rights, and currency convertibility, all of which are crafted along neo-liberal principles with minimal governmental regulation. This global system represents a new phase of capitalism which is "more universal, more unchallenged, more pure and more unadulterated than even before".

For many critics, globalization is essentially an anti-democratic process that excludes the interests of a wide range of groups. But the process is not shaped by market forces alone. It is only made possible by the acquiescence if not active support of governments, especially those in advanced countries.

Governments in developing countries, meanwhile, are often said to be unable to stand up to globalization without incurring severe costs. The government of South Africa, for example, could be punished by capital flight if it insists on implementing its agenda of social reform. The masses of South Africa, however, are likely to sustain heavier costs if the government abandons its reforming mandate. Faced with such a dilemma, governments have generally selected the side of capital for a simple reason.

The list of problems caused by globalization is long. In low-income countries, such as those in Sub-Saharan Africa, where governments have been unable or unwilling to provide their populations with even the most basic protection from the new phase of global capitalism and structural adjustment programmes, the people's plight has been particularly severe.

Opponents of globalization are addressing genuine problems. But it is uncertain whether they will succeed in reversing globalization or even in mitigating its adverse impacts. To begin with, many of them are badly organized. Most of them have also rallied around specific issues instead of articulating a comprehensive counter vision. At this point, the counter vision they project appears to be a global system which is not shaped by the narrow interests of capital but which accommodates the interests of diverse social groups. This vision, however, is not yet well developed.

Further more, these opponents have yet to develop viable strategies to constrain globalization. Some argue for weakening or even abolishing institutions such as the World Bank, the International Monetary Fund, and the World Trade Organization, which they view as agents of globalization, it is unclear why business interests and governments would allow this to happen. The relevance of these bodies is only likely to decline of Third World countries, especially middle-income ones, begin to reduce their dependence of them under pressure from their populations.

Yet the main problem faced by these critics is that many of them do not see the relevance of the state. A successful struggle for genuine popular democracy can liberate the state from the grip of corporate and financial interests, turning it into a critical agent for the promotion of broad social interests. Many NGOs rely instead of civil society, though this cannot substitute the state in policymaking. The struggle against globalization is essentially a struggle for democracy, the state cannot be bypassed, but must be won.

9

Sustainable Tourism Development

Tourism has grown into one of the world's major industries and has thus also become an increasingly important, if complex, issue for environmental policy. Unless it is developed in a sustainable manner, we will be unable to achieve key objectives of global environmental policy such as the preservation of biological diversity, the prevention of climate change or the conservation of natural resources.

Tourism itself depends a lot on the existence of unspoilt nature and landscapes, as well as a healthy environment. If nature is plundered, landscapes are destroyed or water, energy and soil resources are over-exploited, the economic basis of tourism is also undermined. The needs of tourism do therefore overlap with those of environmental protection and nature conservation.

On the one hand, for instance, tourists are becoming increasingly environmentally conscious and are looking to get back to nature and enjoy unspoilt environments when on holiday. On the other hand, however, the number of international tourists is growing constantly. The proportion of long-haul journeys is also increasing steadily, especially in the industrialised nations, where travel is now taken for granted as part of people's lifestyles and has become an important factor in social status. The many different types of travel and holidays are covering more and more countries and regions and, as a result, increasing numbers of previously unspoilt natural environments are being opened up to tourism. This applies equally to coastlines, small islands, coral reefs, rock formations and mountain regions.

There is growing recognition of the need for tourism to develop in a sustainable and environmentally friendly manner. Many countries have, for instance, introduced regulations which require environmental impact surveys to be carried out at least for larger tourist developments. Since the Rio Summit in 1992, there have also been more initiatives in support of sustainable tourism at international level.

- Sustainable tourism allows for the rational use of biological diversity and can contribute to the preservation of that diversity.
- The development of tourism must be controlled and carefully managed so that it remains sustainable.
- Particular attention must be paid to tourism in ecologically and culturally sensitive areas, where mass tourism should be avoided.
- All parties concerned, including in particular the private sector, have a part to play in bringing about the sustainable development of tourism, and voluntary initiatives (codes of conduct, quality labels) should be encouraged.
- Particular importance should be attached to the local level, which is not only responsible for the sustainable development of tourism but should also derive particular benefit from tourism.

It will mark the successful beginning of internationally coordinated efforts to make tourism environmentally and socially sustainable so that many generations to come can continue to experience and enjoy the beauty of nature on our planet.

10

Sustainable Tourism and the Environment

Tourism is high on the international agenda. The 7th session of the Commission on Sustainable Development focused on tourism and subsequently work programmes on sustainable tourism are being developed. Also the Convention on Biological Diversity is embarking on tourism programmes and bilateral and multi-lateral financial institutions placed tourism high on their priority lists. The UN declared 2002 as the international Year of Ecotourism and the World Tourism Organization adopted a Global Code of Ethics for Tourism at its General Assembly, held in Santiago de Chile.

The World Tourism Organization forecasts that there will be 702 million international arrivals in the year 2002, that arrivals will top 1 billion in the year 2010 and that by 2020 and that by 2020 international arrivals will reach 1.6 billion—nearly three times the number of international trips made in 1996, which was 592 million.

Travelers of the 21st century will go farther and farther. The Tourism 2020 Vision forecast predicts that by 2020 one out of every three trips will be a long-haul journey to another region of the world. It is expected that China will become a major force in international tourism and the WTO predicts that about 100 million Chinese will take international trips by 2020, thus putting them in fourth place in numbers of travellers after Germany, Japan and the United States. By the same time, China will attract 137 million visitors—63.5 million overseas visitors travelled to China in 1998 and thus outrank France as the world's top destination. It is estimated that during 1999 France will receive a record number of tourists of more than 70 million; in 2007 France hopes to attract 90 million visitors. The key resource for the most popular tourist destinations is the natural environment: coastal resorts, tropical rainforests, wildlife in national parks and alpine skiresorts, all rely on a mixture of natural beauty, good weather and safe conditions to attract holiday destination is landscape and natural environment, followed by climate, the cost of the journey and the historical features of the place to visit. Hence, conserving the ecological integrity and environment is imperative if tourism is to be sustained.

The pressure from millions of tourists on water and marine resources, on land and landscape, on wildlife and habitat is enormous and often has devastating impact on the environment and the local population who are increasingly deprived of access to clean water and other natural resources.

In some regions, particularly in small island countries, tourism is one of the major reasons for wasting and polluting water: on average one tourist consumes at least 6 times more water than a local resident.

Major water wasters and polluters are golf courses. In many countries, golf has brought heavy ecological and social costs: deforestation, the destruction of bio-diversity and erosion; dispossession of peoples' homes and farms; over-consumption and pollution of water and very high use of pesticides and fertilisers which threaten local residents, workers, wildlife and the golfers themselves. A survey by the Japanese National Doctors Health Insurance Association has revealed that many golfers, caddies and residents living near a golf course suffer from skin inflammation, disorders of the ear, nose and throat and other respiratory illnesses to the inhalation of pesticides because up to 90% of the chemicals sprayed on golf courses end up in the air. In some areas in Thailand, diseases emerged which, prior to the construction of golf courses, had not been known.

In some regions, golf courses have depleted water supply, agricultural production has come to a halt, peasants have become impoverished and forced to migrate to urban areas in search of employment. Golf courses take large amounts of land. It is estimated that each year world wide up to 5,000 hectares of forest are cut to clear land for golf courses.

Very often, the construction of golf courses forms an integral part of a comprehensive tourism project. Adjacent to the golf course, condominiums and/or hotels are built, very often also a marina, an airport and a casino. Studies have shown that such a complex not only has touristic objectives but is often connected to drug trafficking and money-laundering. Even the US State Department has emphasised the link between tourism, money-laundering and offshore banking.

Cruise ships are a major cause for pollution in the Caribbean, destroying maritime life and reefs by releasing waste into the ocean. Recently the Royal Caribbean, the world's second largest cruise line was fined a record sum of US$ 18 million for dumping waste oil and hazardous chemicals into the sea. The company admitted to routinely dumping wasted oil from its fleet and that it deliberately dumped in U.S. harbors and coastal areas many other types of pollutants, including hazardous chemicals from photo processing equipment, dry cleaning shops and printing presses. Some hazardous materials, including toxic solvents from dry cleaning operations, were illegally placed in the garbage abroad the ships. The material was then either incinerated on the ship or dumped in U.S. or foreign ports mixed with ordinary garbage.

It was announced that the Royal Caribbean Cruise reported a profit of US$ 338 million in 1997, a 93% increase over the previous year, Carnival Corporation's Holland, the biggest cruise company with a turnover of US$ 3 billion in 1997 made a net profit of US $836 million, 25% more than in 1996. Both cruise companies have recently been fined millions of dollars for dumping untreated bilge water, oil and other waste into Alaskan waters.

However, the impact of oil and hazardous waste on water, maritime life and coral reefs is devastating and all fines paid for the damage caused by the cruise ships will not revive dead corals.

A recent Green peace study on coral reefs-one of the marine world's great natural treasures-predicts that the coral bleaching which dramatically whitened many of the world's reefs last year will escalate rapidly under accepted global climate models and that the damage would wreak havoc in fisheries and tourism, disrupting the economies of many nations.

A WWF study recently published on "Climate Change and its Impacts on Tourism", warned that droughts; rising seas, flash floods, forest fires and diseases could turn profitable destinations into holiday horror stories. The report urges the tourist industry to persuade western industrialised governments to take more concerted action to reduce their nations' carbon dioxide emissions the main cause of global warming.

The Need for Action and Education

If governments, the international community and the tourism industry want to save the world's major tourist destinations, immediate action is required. Governments and the tourism industry must abide to the principle that environmental protection is an integral part of tourism development. In order to protect the environment and mitigate the damages caused by tourism, some countries have decided to take action: The Spanish island Minorca and the Seychelles will introduce Eco-tax on tourism. This tax will be around US $ 12 per person in Minorca and its revenues are earmarked for the maintenance of national parks and the restoration of damaged coastline. Visitors to the Seychelles will have to buy a so-called "gold-card" at a price of 100$ which entitles unlimited access to the country; income from this card will be used for sewage management and protection of fresh water supply.

Only if tourism investors and developers:

(a) consider the natural capacity for the regeneration and future productivity of natural resources:

(*b*) recognise the contribution that people and communities, customs and life styles, make to the tourism experience and therefore accept that these people must have an equitable share in the economic benefits of tourism; and

(*c*) listen to local people in the tourist destinations, tourism may become sustainable.

Education and awareness raising campaigns at all levels are therefore imperative.

11

Sustainable Tourism—Illusion or Realistic Alternative?

We find them in the big cities of the world and in the most remote jungles; they cross the deserts of Africa and cruise to see the penguins along the polar ice caps; they climb the Himalayan mountains and dive deep into the coral seas of tropical oceans. Tourists are every where these days—easily recognisable by their cameras and camcorders, their leisure-time outfit, and their unsatiable desire to get away from home and experience life with a difference.

Tourism has become the biggest industry in the world. If offers jobs for 200 million people and contributes 11.7 per cent to global Gross National Product. Almost 700 million tourist arrivals are expected for this year, and this number is estimated to grow to 1.5 billion by the year 2020.

Most countries in the world, with very few exceptions, compete with each other to get as large a share as possible of the huge cake which is up for distribution. Attracting tourists, especially from beyond the own borders, means foreign exchange earnings and jobs and income for the local people. But the list of possible draw backs, especially for developing countries, is along: the environment and natural beauty may be harmed by infrastructure and hotel buildings; the intrusion of large numbers of foreigners with little knowledge and respect for the local culture and tradition may cause social tensions; there may be an upsurge of prostitution and sex-related diseases; and the local economy may be disrupted because labor is siphoned off from farming of the tourism sector, and the high purchasing power of tourists may promote inflation.

People concerned over these undesirable side-effects of tourism have, there fore, invented the term of 'soft' tourism-one which would impact less on the society and environment of the host country. The latest catchwords are 'sustainable' tourism or 'eco-tourism' suggesting that tourism can be organised in such a way that it does not harm the environment and local culture. But are we not deceiving ourselves if we believe that tourism in its modern forms can be 'sustainable'? Sustainable according to the widely used definition of the Brundtlandt Commission means "meeting the needs of the present without compromising the ability of future generations to meet their own needs".

This entails, for instance, that we try to avoid the possible effects of climate change which is caused by greenhouse gas emissions into the atmosphere. Tourism, because of the enormous increase in air and road traffic, is a major factor in polluting the atmosphere, increasing CO2 emissions, and damaging the protective ozone layer, also, increased traffic as a result of tourism used up additional non-renewal resources such as petrol and kerosene and adds to air pollution in overcrowded cities or in frequented tourist regions. Needless to argue that the term 'sustainable' could hardly be applied in this connection, especially in view of that fact that tourist numbers are going to double in the next 20 years.

Also tourism is by no means more 'sustainable' if tourists leave their ghettos and begin to interact with the local population. As long as only a few open-minded people seek to submerge themselves in the culture and society of the host country this may lead to more interaction and inter-cultural understanding. But just imagine what would happen if all the Japanese and Americans visiting Paris, Rome or Berlin during the summer would come knocking at the door of local people to learn more about their real life. Or if all the Germans on the beaches of Thailand would decide that travelling with a backpack through the country's villages was more rewarding than staying in a luxurious hotel. Then it would soon turn out that such a form of tourism was even less 'sustainable' than organised travel in its present form.

The only truly 'sustainable' form of tourism, therefore, would be to stay at home and to avoid additional resource consumption. For obvious reasons, this is no realistic alternative and, if consistently applied, would lead to a world economic crisis. Instead of using the illusionary term 'sustainable' tourism, we should, therefore, speak more often about 'responsible' tourism. This term implies that we try to keep the negative environmental and cultural impacts of tourism at a minimum while making sure that benefits go to the poor, especially in developing countries. 'Responsible' tourism is not against travelling, but it takes care that landscapes are not destroyed, natural and architectural beauties preserved, foreign cultures respected, and economic benefits spread as widely as possible. 'Responsible' tourism has the advantage that corresponds both to the wishes of most tourists—who want to stay in a clean environment with a clean conscience and the interests of the local people who derive jobs and incomes from it. But it needs a strong state which is able to enforce environmental regulations, suppress corruption and make sure that income from tourism benefits the whole country and not only a few national or international entrepreneurs.

To travel and to experience the world is an age-old dream which more and more people in the richer parts of the world are able to fulfil for themselves. But the tourism boom threatens to become self-destructive if it continues to expand without fetters. 'Responsible' tourism strikes a balance between the needs of the environment, the respect for the other cultures, and the wish of modern people to live in a world without borders. However, it is an illusion to believe that mass tourism with 1.5 billion arrivals per year could truly be sustainable.

12

Pro-Poor Tourism

Opportunities for Sustainable Local Development

Tourism is the world's largest industry, with over 10 percent of GDP globally directly related to tourism activities. Rising standards of living in the countries of the North, declining long-haul travel costs, increasing holiday entitlements, changing demographics and strong consumer demand for exotic international travel have resulted in significant tourism growth to developing countries. Tourism is the principal export for one third of developing countries. Tourism brings relatively powerful consumers to Southern countries, potentially an important market for local entrepreneurs and an engine for local sustainable economic development. There is no reliable data on domestic tourism but it is growing rapidly in South America and in China and South East Asia; it represents a very significant economic opportunity for many local communities.

Tourism and Aid

Multilateral and bilateral aid agencies are wary of involving themselves in the tourism sector. In 1969 the World Bank created a Tourism Projects Department recognising that in the Mediterranean and Adriatic countries, and in Mexico, tourism had been a significant generator of foreign exchange and of direct and indirect employment, internationally in the late nineteen sixties, there was considerable concern about high rates of unemployment and the ability of developing countries to service debt. Tourism sector studies were completed in some 31 countries and tourism staff regularly participated in World Bank macro-economic missions—their reports focussed on the potential for growth in tax revenues, foreign exchange earnings and direct and indirect employment effects. The primary emphasis was on national economic impact. By 1978 when the World Bank closed its Tourism Projects Department of the Bank had provided loans and credits for 18 projects in 14 countries and it was the major source of funds and technical assistance for tourism development. The bank withdrew from tourism development for a range of reasons amongst which were anxieties about the role of the bank in funding projects of develop luxury hotels designed to attract wealthy travellers from the developed countries. This strategy was seen inconsistent with new policy objectives which prioritised the bottom 40 per cent, the Bank's priorities were shifting towards the poor, a group, which was gaining relatively little from tourism development. There was a growing literature that focussed on the negative economic, social and cultural impacts of unmanaged tourism on local communities. The fuel crises of the nineteen seventies also undermined some of the forecasts that had been made for the strength of the market and the Bank withdrew from the sector in parallel with most other multilateral and bilateral agencies.

The international agencies followed a macro-economic tourism agenda in the nineteen seventies and eighties focussing on tax and foreign exchange revenues at the national level, major hotel and resort development, international promotion and national and regional master planning all attracted funding. In the nineties the adoption of the new poverty elimination target of halving the number of people living on less than 1 US $ per day by 2015 refocused development assistance on pro-poor growth. Multilateral and bilateral aid agency agendas are shifting towards micro economic growth strategies, which benefit local communities and in particular those below the poverty threshold. With poverty elimination now at the heart of decision aid, the potential for using tourism to generate pro-poor economic growth is being reassessed.

Since the mid-1980s, interest in 'green' tourism, eco-tourism and community tourism has grown rapidly among tour operators, policy makers, advocates and researchers. All of these focus on the need to ensure that tourism does not erode the environmental and cultural base on which it depends. The emphasis has been on minimising social, cultural and environmental impacts; rather than on positively affecting the livelihoods of the poor.

The Potential of Pro-Poor Tourism

There are a number of reasons to look again at tourism and to assess its potential to generate pro-poor growth. 80 per cent of the world's poor live in just 12 countries and tourism is significant or growing in all but one of them. Tourism is a very large sector, it is growing rapidly, and there is some evidence that it is relatively labour intensive. The consumer travels to the destination, creating additional—local—opportunities for the sale of additional goods and services—ranging from local pottery to a guided walk. Tourism can be used to diversify local economies; it can often be developed in remote and marginal areas with few other diversifications or export opportunities. These areas often attract tourists because of their high landscape, cultural and wildlife values. These natural resources and the local culture are amongst the few assets of the poor.

Pro-poor tourism generates net benefits for the poor. It can be defined as forms of tourism where the benefits to the poor are greater than costs which tourism brings them. Economic costs and benefits are clearly important but social environmental and cultural costs and benefits are clearly important, but social and benefits also need to be taken into account. Pro-poor tourism aims to expand opportunities for those living on less than 1 US$ per day. Whilst it will also need to be sustainable preserving local culture, minimizing environmental impacts, it will be driven by the poverty agenda. Community-based tourism seeks to promote initiatives by local communities or individuals within them; much has been learnt from these projects. Maximizing the poverty elimination effect requires that the emphasis is placed on involving those people who are living on less than 1 US$ per day and creating economic opportunities for them. Not all community tourism is pro-poor in this sense.

Effects on the Livelihoods of the Poor

Assessing the livelihood impacts of tourism is not simply a matter of counting jobs or wage income. Participatory poverty assessments demonstrate great variety in the priorities of the poor and factors affecting livelihood security and sustainability. Tourism can affect many of these, positively and negatively, often indirectly. It is important to assess these impacts and their distribution.

Tourism can generate four different types of local cash income generally involving different categories of people:

- wages from formal employment;
- earnings from selling goods, services, or casual labour (e.g., food, crafts, building materials, guide services);
- and profits arising from locally owned enterprises
- Income: this may include profits from a community run enterprise, dividends from a private sector partnership and land rental paid by an investor.

Waged employment can be sufficient to lift a household from insecure to secure. But it may only be an available to a minority, and not to the poor. Casual earnings per person may be very small, but much more widely spread and may be enough, for instance, to cover school fees for one or more children. Work as a tourist guide although casual, is often of high status and relatively well paid. There are relatively few examples of successful and sustainable collective income from tourism.

Negative economic impacts include inflation, dominance by outsiders in land markets and in-migration, which erodes economic opportunities for the local poor. Impacts differ between men and women. Women can be the first to suffer from loss of natural resources (e.g., access to fuel wood) and cultural/sexual exploitation, but may benefit most from physical infrastructure improvements (e.g. piped water or a grinding mill) where this is a by-product of tourism.

Positive Development Impacts of Tourism

On the positive side, tourism can generate funds for investment in health, education and other assets, provide infrastructure, stimulate development of social capital, strengthen sustainable management of natural resources, and create a demand for improved assets (especially education). On the negative side, tourism can reduce local access to natural resources draw heavily upon local infrastructure, and disrupt social networks.

Tourism affects the livelihoods of the poor by changing their access to assets. In several cases, tourism's impact on people's access to natural resources or physical infrastructure has been identified as the most important benefit or concern.

Cultural Impacts of Tourism can be Positive or Negative

Local residents often highlight the way tourism affects other livelihood goals-whether positively or negatively—such as cultural pride, a sense of control, good health, and reduced vulnerability. Socio-cultural intrusion by tourists is often cited as a negative impact. Certainly sexual exploitation particularly affects the poorest women, girls and young men. The poor themselves may view other types of cultural change as positive. Tourism can also increase the value attributed to minority cultures by national policy-makers. Overall, the cultural impacts of tourism are hard to disentangle from wider processes of development.

The overall balance of positive and negative livelihood impacts will vary enormously between situations, among people and over time, and particularly in the extent to which local priorities are able to influence the planning process. The application of a 'sustainable' livelihood framework is essential to developing pro-poor approaches. The distribution of livelihood impacts has to be considered. The poor are far from being a homogenous group. The positive and negative impacts of tourism will inevitably be distributed unevenly among poor groups, reflecting different patterns of assets, activities, opportunities and choices. The most substantial benefits, particularly jobs, may be concentrated among few. Net benefits are likely to be smallest, or negative, for the poorest.

Policies to Enhance Pro-Poor Tourism

Despite innumerable case studies of tourism development, there is relatively little assessment of practical experience in strategies to make tourism more pro-poor. Nevertheless, lessons can be drawn from a wealth of small initiatives (many from 'community tourism' or 'conservation and development' programmes), supplemented by expanding knowledge on 'pro-poor growth strategies', several policy implications clearly emerge.

1. *Put Poverty Issues on the Tourism Agenda*

A first step is to recognise that enhancing the poverty impacts of tourism is different from commercial, environmental or ethical concerns. PPT can be incorporated as an additional objective, but this requires pro-active and strategic intervention. There may well be trade-offs to make-for example between attracting all-inclusive operators and maximising informal sector opportunities, or between faster growth through outside investment, and slower growth building on local capacity. These trade-offs need to be addressed.

2. *Enhance Economic Opportunities and a Wide Range of Impacts*

Two approaches need to be combined:

- Expand poor people's economic participation by addressing the barriers they face, and maximising a wide range of employment, self-employment and informal sector opportunities;
- Incorporate wider concerns of the poor into decision-making. Reducing competition for natural resources, minimising trade-offs with other livelihood activities, using tourism to create physical infrastructure that benefits the poor and addressing cultural disruption will often be particularly important.

3. *A Multi-Level Approach*

Pro-poor interventions can and should be taken at three different levels:

- this is where pro-active practical partnerships can be developed between operators, residents, NGOs and local authorities, to maximise benefits;
- national policy level-policy reform may be needed on a range of tourism issues (planning, licensing, training) and non-tourism issues (land tenure, business incentives, infrastructure, land-use planning);
- International level-to encourage responsible consumer and business behaviour, and to enhance commercial codes of conduct.

4. *Work Though Partnerships, Including Business and Tourists*

National and local governments, private enterprises, industry associations, NGOs, community organisations, consumers, and donors all have a role to play. It is particularly important to engage business, and to ensure that initiatives are commercially realistic and integrated into main stream operations. Private operators will not be able to devote substantial time and resources to developing pro-poor actions. NGOs and donors can help in reducing the transaction costs of changing commercial practice—for example, facilitating the training, organisation, and communication that would enable businesses to use more local suppliers. Changing the attitudes of tourists (at both international and national levels) is also essential if pro-poor tourism is to be commercially viable and sustainable.

5. *Incorporate Pro-Poor Tourism Approaches into Mainstream Tourism*

Pro-poor tourism should not just be pursued in niche markets (such as eco-tourism or community tourism). It is even more important that mass tourism is developed in ways that benefit the poor. It is also important to assess which tourism segments are particularly relevant to the poor. Domestic tourists are likely to be important customers.

6. *Reform Decision-Making Systems*

It is impossible to prescribe exactly how each tourism enterprise should develop in ways that best fit with livelihoods. The most important principle is to enhance the participation of the poor. Three different ways of doing this can be identified:

- Strengthen rights at local level (e.g., tenure over tourism assets), so that local people have market power and make their own decisions over developments.
- Develop more participatory planning.
- Use planning gain and other incentives to encourage private investors to enhance local benefits. These approaches require implementation capacity among governmental and non-governmental institutions within the destination, and require a supportive national policy framework.

It is time to reconsider the role of tourism in contributing to pro-poor development. Tourism should be judged against other possible strategies and where it offers the best opportunities for pro-poor growth, or where it can make a useful contribution by increasing the diversity of opportunities for the poor, tourism it should be considered. However, careful and effective local management will be essential if it is to contribute to meeting poverty targets and if tourism dependency is to be avoided.

13

The Biggest Industry the World has Ever Seen: The Future of World Tourism

The year 2020 will see the penetration of technology into all aspects of life. it will become possible to live one's days without exposure to other people, according to WTO's latest look into the future.

But this bleak prognosis has a silver lining for the tourism sector. People in the high-tech future will crave the human touch and tourism will be the principal means to achieve this.

Tourism companies that manage to provide "high-touch" products will prosper. Upscale, luxury services that pamper and spoil their customers have a bright future in the upcoming century. But WTO's report also predicts good prospects for low-budget destinations and packages. Self-catering holiday facilities, for example, which offer plenty of opportunities for socializing among families and fiends. Opportunities abound at both ends of the spectrum and there will be plenty of them.

$5 billion a Day Industry

WTO's study Tourism: 2020 Vision predicts 1.5 billion tourists will be visiting foreign countries annually by the year 2020, spending more that US$2 trillion-or US$5 billion every day. These forecasts represent nearly three times more international tourists than the 66m million recorded in 1999 and nearly five times more tourism spending, which last year topped US$453 billion. Tourist arrivals are predicted to grow by an average 4.3 per cent a year over the next two decades, while receipts from international tourism will climb by 6.7 per cent a year.

To factor in domestic tourism, WTO multiplies arrivals by 10 and quadruples receipts, which brings us to the grant totals of 16 billion tourists spending US$8 trillion in 2020.

Tourism in the 21st century will not only be the world's biggest industry, it will be the largest by far that the world has ever seen. Along with its phenomenal growth and size, the tourism industry will also have to take on more responsibility for its extensive impacts. Not only its economic impact, but also its impact on the environment, on societies and on cultural sites, all of which will be increasingly scrutinized by governments, consumer groups and the travelling public.

Will hope that Tourism 2020 Vision will be more than a useful marketing tool, that it will act as a warning signal for destinations-helping them recognize the need to prepare for the pressure of growth, TWO is advising destinations to implement long-term, strategic planning and to strengthen the partnerships, both strategically and at the operational level, between the public and private sectors.

Growth of Long-haul

Tourism: 2020 Vision indicates that tourists of the 21st century will travelling further afield on their holidays, often to China and even to outer space. The percentage of long-haul travel is predicted to increase from 18 per cent in 1995 to 24 per cent by 2020.

Tourism companies looking to cash in on this booming sector are advised to look towards Asia. China will be the world's number one destination by the year 2020 and it will also become the fourth most important generating market. Currently it does not even figure among the world's destinations predicted to make great strides in the tourism industry are Russia, Hong Kong, Thailand, Singapore, Indonesia and South Africa.

Short pleasure voyages to outer space will become a reality by 2004 or 2005, according to the study carried out by WTO Statistics Chief Enzo Paci in consultation with 85 governments and 50 tourism visionaries.

It is expected space trips will last up to four days and cost on average US$100,000. NASA, the US space agency, has recently surveyed the travel industry for interest in space tourism and some US companies are already taking reservations and deposits from private citizens hoping to become the first tourists in outer space.

But while some travellers may be suiting up for space voyages, the vast majority of the world's population will never leave their own countries, not even by the year 2020.

Only 7 percent of the world's population will be travelling internationally by the year 2020, up from 3.5 per cent in 1996-but still just the tip of the iceberg.

European Trends

"Tourism: 2020 Vision" predicts that Europe will remain by far the leading inbound tourism region as well as the main generator of international tourists. International arrivals in Europe will reach 717 million by 2020? more than twice as many as last year.

Overall, tourism to Europe is predicted to grow more slowly than the world average; at a rate of 3.1 per cent annually, though some countries will fare better than others. Central and Eastern European countries will become the new motor for Europe, feeding and being fed by other European and long-haul generating markets. Tourism to Central and Eastern Europe will grow by 4.8 per cent a year and the former Soviet Block countries will surpass 200 million arrivals by 2016—a doubling in last 15 years.

The Eastern Mediterranean countries of Cyprus, Turkey and Israel are also expected to show good growth of 4.6 per cent a year. Tourism to the United Kingdom is forecast to grow by 4 per cent annually, just under the world average. Reflecting world patterns and increasing air travel, Europeans will be taking trips more frequently and further from home. Total outbound travel from European countries is predicted to reach 771 million trips a year by 2010, again more than twice as many as last year.

Long-haul travel to countries outside of Europe will grow by 6.1 per cent a year in the upcoming decades to reach 15 per cent of all trips taken by Europeans or 115,600,000 departures. Long-haul currently accounts for 12 per cent of European outbound travel or about 42 million trips a year.

Since the typical European tourist who spends his holiday at the beach will be more frequently choosing Asian or Caribean resorts, European beach destinations are advised to orientate their product development and marketing increasingly to new tourist sources, especially Japan, the newly industrialized countries of Asia and the Americas.

Mature European destinations will have continually to strive to seek product and market differentiation to avoid a tired or stale image in major generating markets.

Recipe for Success

While growth of the tourism industry will be unstoppable in the 21st century, increased benefits cannot be taken for granted. Competition among destinations will also become increasingly fierce.

The study Tourism: 2020 Vision outlines a series of 12 megatrends that will shape the sector and offers advice on how to better compete. No destination or tourism operator can afford to sit back and wait for more tourists to arrive. They have to be won-and there will be winners and losers. To be a winner, there are a number of imperatives:

1. Development focused on quality and sustainability.
2. Value-for-money.
3. Full utilization of information technology to identify and communicate effectively with market segments and niches.

Product development and marketing will need to match each other more closely, based on the main travel motivators of the 21st century. Tourism: 2020 Vision calls these motivating factors the Three E's-Entertainment, Excitement and Education.

The study also highlights the importance of image in a tourists' selection of a holiday destination in the future. While an image of safety and security is already an important deciding factor for tourists, holiday makers of the 21st century will be looking for places with a trendy image.

As 2020 Vision points out, the next century will mark the emergence the tourism destinations as 'a fashion accessory'. The choice of holiday destination will help define the identity of the travellers and, in an increasingly homogeneous world, set him apart from the hordes of other tourists.

Boutique destinations and space agencies beware! You are on the threshold of meeting the 21st century tourist.

(14)

The Tourism Juggernaut

Tourism, already one of the world's biggest industries, is expected to treble in size by the year 2010. Now, concern about tourism's impact on fragile environments and cultures is leading to serious attempts to make it more 'sustainable'.

"Getting away from it all," is understandably popular. With so many wonderful places in the world, prices of international travel falling, and the stresses and strains of everyday life increasing, more people are traveling.

"The sustained growth since the beginning of this decade and the acceleration now underway proves that tourism is one of the world's most durable and dynamic economic sectors." But around every silver lining, there is always a cloud, and as tourism grows, so too do the criticisms. Evidence of the downside of tourism-culturally, environmentally and economically-is now such that tourism has become a dirty word amongst many communities, environmental groups, and human rights campaigners.

Tourism's vociferous appetite for basic resources-land, water and energy-has meant that the tourism industry and governments are increasingly finding themselves opposed over land rights and water rights by local people. One of the most famous long-term tourism protests has been in Goa. With one five-star hotel consuming as much water as five local villages and one five-star tourist consuming 28 times more electricity per day than a local Goan, local discontent over resource-use is understandable.

Lack of access by locals to public beaches, violation by hotels of environmental regulations, and heavy-handed tactics by local authorities to free-up beach areas for hotel's use, have all been cited in legal disputes throughout the world. Commercialization of culture and destruction of traditional lifestyles also became commonplace.

Tourism is also cited in terms of gross human rights abuse. In Burma, the military junta has forcibly moved millions of people from their homes to make room for tourism development, and used hundreds of thousands as forced labour on tourism-related projects. Such problems are often brushed aside by the tourism industry and by governments, who cite the economic bonuses behind promoting tourism.

But as foreign exchange leakages from developing to developed countries equal around 60 to 75 per cent, and local jobs are generally menial and low-paid, the economic benefits are often skewed away from destination countries. This is particularly the case in destinations which receive a lot of cheap, package tours.

Sustainable tourism is defined as: "Tourism and associated infrastructures that: operate within capacities for the regeneration and future productivity of natural resources, recognize the contribution of local people and their cultures, accept that these people must have an equitable share in the economic benefits of tourism, and are guided by the wishes of local people and communities in the destination areas."

Such a definition seems reasonable, but as with the 'sustainable development' of any industry'—to implement it is more difficult, particularly in developing countries. How can a country set limits on the numbers of tourists it accepts when it desperately needs foreign exchange to pay off foreign debts and fuel economic growth? How can local people receive an equitable share of tourism's profits when there is no way they can compete with the foreign multinational hotels and tour operators on price, and do not have the same international marketing networks? And how can developers be forced to consult with a representative sample of local people, and not just the business elite?

At the nub of sustainable tourism are issues of equity and local control-issues that it is almost impossible for the tourism industry to address because of their need to maximise profit. Changes are occurring, but they tend to be in simpler areas such as environmental management. Efforts are being made by the hotel industry for instance, to encourage responsible water, waste and energy management, which includes a wide range of techniques including extensive recycling, water and energy conservation and uses of alternative energy, such as solar power.

15

Tourism and the Environment

The relationship between tourism and the environment is obvious, and is largely established through what is sometimes called "environment quality". This quality is perceived in different ways according to the human population and the circumstances presiding tourist activities at any given moment. Any analysis of the relationship between tourism and the environment that we can include under human ecology therefore comprises aspects of the natural sciences as well as the social sciences.

Tourist activity is promoted, conditioned and influenced by the environmental circumstances of each region and can be affected by modifications or changes in those circumstances. Although a lot of emphasis has been placed on the negative impact or modifications in "environment quality" attributed to tourism, it is also accepted that it can be a very important factor in the preservation and defence of ecological values threatened by more destructive alternatives for the use of territory. Very often, tourism can be the most suitable and most satisfactory way of using a region's renewable natural resources. Nevertheless, their management and use need to be properly regulated so as to guarantee their renewability and persistence.

There is room in this complex field of relations to study, rationalize and optimize an activity as important as tourism, from the point of view of its insertion in the ecological systems with which it interacts. However, there are relatively few efficient studies on issues of real importance. It is startling to observe that places with tourist potential undertake little or no research in this field.

One possible cause is the difficulty in identifying the real problematic in tourism/environment relations, which is essentially interdisciplinary and involves the integration of traditionally separate areas of knowledge. Although work is undertaken from time to time on environmental psychology, the sociology of tourism, behaviour in relation to the environment, etc., they are very rarely combined with works on the environment, forestry and agricultural policies, soil use, contamination, biodiversity, evaluation of environmental impact, nature conservation, etc., in search for a more integrated management of tourist resources.

Responsible Tourism

Tourism runs the risk of going the way of other phenomena, which first of all experience rapid growth and then suffer a spectacular collapse, what in Economics is often called "boom and bust".

The causes are familiar: a certain dose of greed, often based on a lack of mid-or long-term planning, property speculation, little consideration for local populations—in both economic and social aspects—and, in general, a lack of awareness as regards environmental aspects—contamination, water use, energy, etc.,—on the part of tour operators, hoteliers and other agents involved in tourism in its different forms, including the tourists themselves. The problem is particularly evident in ecotourism, abased on the wonders of the natural world: landscapes, flora and fauna. Many expert fear for the future of this type of tourism, which has grown spectacularly in the last few years. Landscapes deteriorate, the fauna decreases, the designers and administrators of tourist developments fail to respect the most elementary principles for adapting architecture to its surroundings, or else there is little effort to recycle, economize or educate with a few honourable exceptions, tourist planning is careless and irresponsible.

And yet a responsible approach would be in the tour operators' own interests, as it would make the tourist industry sustainable, with positive influences on biological, economic and social aspects.

Ecotourism, for example, has shown that when properly conceived it can become a powerful instrument for the preservation of nature, with very favourable repercussions for local populations and for educational programmes, while offering hundreds of millions of ecotourists a wide range of spiritual and physical satisfactions. At the same time, the host countries can take pride in what they have to offer their citizens and the rest of the world.

The preventive and corrective measures are known to us; what is needed is a sense of responsibility and farsightedness on the part both of the authorities and of the industry. We need regulations and controls, so as to put the people who do the damage out of circulation and reward those at the forefront of sustainability.

Sustainable Tourism

After several decades of rapid quantitative growth, tourism is going through a period of profound transformation, Tourists, the consumers in this industry, but also the public, have started to demand a change in the conditions of production and use of tourist services, putting an end to the uncontrolled expansion of mass tourism.

This is the ultimate reason, apart from ethical and aesthetic considerations, why tourist activity as a whole, in the private sector as well as in the public and voluntary (NGO) sector, has begun to seriously analyse the implications of tourism in terms of socio-cultural and environmental impacts, and to consider the need to draw up and implement environment friendly tourist policies.

Indeed, while not denying the viability and the utility of alternative approaches of an external and coercive nature, it is obvious that the decision-makers in the sector react better to positive stimuli. The realisation that their clients prefer well-conserved areas and non-aggressive tourist practices and that they are prepared to pay more for this makes it easier to adopt strategies of sustainability in the tourist industry in a sincere alliance with conservation movements.

All this points to the validity of Overall Quality Management as a viable method in sustainable tourist activities. The overall quality approach renders the management of products and especially of tourist areas extremely sensitive to the preferences and expectations of consumers. The private public profitability of a tourist destination will depend on clients' satisfaction, since these will return more often and for longer and will pass on a positive image of their holiday experiences. In so far as these preferences and expectations include the demand for unspoilt settings, consumer satisfaction, and therefore the profitability of a tourist spot, will call for the development of strategies for sustainable development.

One can believe this is a productive approach for sustainability in the tourist business and one that makes for professional attitudes that fit in with the economic targets of businesses and other organisations. There is only one prior requirement: continued education and training of everyone involved in tourism, from consumers to those responsible for tourist policies. The demand for quality, and even more so for environmental quality, is a call to people's awareness, to their understanding of the environmental and cultural implications of any activity and their ability to express themselves and to organise to choose the most clear-sighted line of action.

Tourism in the Modern Age

What will the tourist trade of the year 2000 be like? Who will be the tourists of the coming millennium? These are the questions which, faced with the extraordinary boom in tourism, experts, tour operators and politicians have repeatedly posed over the last fifteen years. These questions arise either because of the financial profits the tourist industry involves, or from the demands of consumers who show new awarenesses, habits and lifestyles. In the eighties mass tourism gradually changed and people began to talk of "tourisms". Expressions such as cultural tourism, sports tourism, religious tourism, adventure tourism or ecotourism have become part of everyday language. In the past, the dominant practice was to take one long holiday in a single destination; today, people tend to distribute their holidays over different destinations and different times of the year.

From a socio-historical point of view, three types of tourist industry can be differentiated. In the case of the industrial tourist, for whom work is the center of existence, the motivations for travelling can be summed up as rest and freedom from responsibilities. This type is gradually decreasing in number. The hedonistic tourist belongs to the generation that discovered entertainment and consumerism. They like to go on holiday to experiment, to explore the unknown, enjoy themselves meet other people and relax in unspoilt natural surroundings. These are the majority today and will continue to be so. Finally, the modern age tourist, someone who tends to reduce the polarity between work and play: not just work, but just not fun, either. Their reasons for travelling include broadening their personal horizons and getting back to simple things and nature, with a touch of creativity in the planning of their journey. These are gradually growing in number and in future will form an important segment of demand.

One characteristic in the expectations of the modern age tourist is the capacity to make a critical appraisal of the offer and to influence it. Producers should be more attentive and sensitive to the new demands and be flexible enough to cater for the tourist in search of higher quality. In the third millennium in fact, the concept of quality will have to take environmental aspects more into account. Recent forms of tourism point to a renewed interest in nature and a wish for quality tourism. So much so, that some tourist spots are reorganising their own offer in keeping with these trends. Quality is the result of a complex strategy which is organised day by day. The consumers, whose environmental awareness is constantly growing, will expect to identify, verify and be able to differentiate ecologically correct products from the imitations now invading the market.

The present millennium is coming to a end and is leaving Western countries with a high level of welfare and a large tourist demand to satisfy. Nevertheless, serious environmental problems also plague areas that receive a high influx of tourists. Tourists, tour operators, local authorities and the general public are therefore called on to find new forms of coexistence and the right solutions for themselves and for the survival of the planet.

16

Economics and Sustainable Development

Economists and ecologists were once seen as enemies: environmental protection, it was thought, could only be achieved at the expense of economic growth. The misconception persists at the extremes among both the most fundamentalist Greens and the most ideological free marketers. But increasingly it is now being recognized that development and care for the environment go hand in hand. This interdependence is coalescing in the new and necessary discipline of environmental economics.

Conventional economics patterns have often assumed that growth and technical progress will nullify all resource and environmental limits. Environmental economics recognizes that the world's natural capital underpins all development, and that it is rapidly becoming scarcer as human demands exceed the globe's long-term carrying capacity. Government of India has introduced environmental measures over the last two decades, but need to move further towards integrating them into economic policies. There can be no real sustainable development unless environment and development policies are integrated at the very beginning of the decision-making process.

Quantifying the Environmental Cost

One of the first steps is to work out the true costs of polluting and depleting the World's natural resources, such as its soil, air and water, the climate and the ozone layer. These have often been regarded as free goods, and it was believed that the world has an infinite capacity to absorb the effects of human activities. Environmental economists, recognizing that the social and economic costs of degradation are very great, are trying to quantify them. They say that this will make possible better use of such tools as cost-benefit analysis, environmental impact assessment and risk assessment—and the production of national income accounts which reflect the depletion and degradation of natural resources. As these costs are identified and quantified, economic policy can increasingly be developed with sustainable development as the primary objective. Achieving sustainable development requires industrialized and developing countries to make dramatic changes in national and international policies based on a global partnership. The greenhouse effect, the destruction of the ozone layer, the extinction of species and contamination of the oceans, and other environmental problems, affect us all, no matter which corner of the global we inhabit.

The first and essential step in overcoming a difficulty is to recognize it and understand it. Concern over the difficulties related to sustainability has led scientists and national and international institutions to study the concept and suggest ways of meeting its many requirements. Indicators have been established to measure pollution levels, soil erosion, salinization, deforestation and a host of environmental problems. Evaluating the impact of such natural resource-use on ecosystems is a major step towards finding the necessary solutions.

For example, it has become clear, on a macroeconomic level, that national accounting systems fail to reflect these effects adequately. Deterioration of the world's rivers, land degradation, air pollution and contamination of the seas are not taken into consideration. Inadequate accounting distorts reality and gives a false idea of the true consequences of growth and production.

On a microeconomic level, much is being done to redefine production costs. Incorporating the cost of waste management and internalizing negative external impacts within production prices are beneficial aspects of the economics of sustainability.

Steps are being taken to evaluate public and commonly held assets and to put a price on them, even though they may not be subject to market forces. These are only in the earliest stage but they will allow for more accurate evaluation of the world's natural capital. Fiscal, market, quota and other instruments are being developed to enforce change in the way in which certain resources are used. Examples include markets for transferable emission quotas or compensatory taxation mechanisms designed to ensure that economic forces act to reduce greenhouse gas emissions. Efforts at impact analysis—and in a general sense, cost-benefit analysis—permit rough estimations of the impact that projects might have on ecosystems.

Long-term Repercussions

These instruments carry significant limitations but they are important nevertheless because they attempt to quantify impacts on the natural world and to achieve a more rational use of natural resources. The development of such instruments and evaluation techniques will have significant repercussions in the formulation of sustainable long-term policies. But we must bear in mind that sustainability is not just an economic issue: it is also a political and cultural one.

The concept of sustainability demands as alternative view point in which humankind and the natural world are perceived as a unit—as different yet mutually sustaining aspects of a whole. This perception is not incompatible with progress. It does not renounce development. It simply seeks to affirm life and refuses to discriminate between the means and the end. It understands that happiness cannot be achieved by destructive means. The questions of how to produce and how to consume therefore become extremely important. Neither should be at the expense of the future or of the natural world. Efficiency is not limited to the links between investment, products and prices: it must address the rational use of resources, including environmental and cultural consequences, both in the long-and the short-term.

Very considerable adjustments must be made in the interests of sustainable development. They demand a reassessment of all our activities which cannot, logically, be done overnight. It is a long and continuous process, characterized by steadfastness and compromise.

17

Forests—The Earth's Lungs

The world's forest cover is shrinking. Over the past 50 years nearly half of the world's original forest cover has been lost—some 3 billion hectares. Each year another 16 million hectares of virgin forest are cut, bulldozed, or burned.

Between 1980 and 1995 the world lost some 180 million hectares of forest—an area the size of Indonesia. While developed countries had a net increase of 20 million hectares due to reforestation, this gain was more than offset by a net decrease of 200 million hectares in the developing world.

Forests have many functions of value both to humanity and to nature itself. Take away the trees, and the intricately linked ecosystem unravels. Forests absorb carbon dioxide and produce oxygen, anchor soils, regulate the water cycle, protect against erosion, and provide a habitat for millions of species.

Forest products are essential to the world economy, worth about US$ 400 billion annually in timber, pulp, paper, and fuel wood. Forest products other than wood, such as medicines, vegetables, and fruits, provide another US$ 20 billion and are growing in importance.

Healthy forests boost food production. Trees soak up and store water from season to season, slowly releasing moisture during dry periods. Without tree cover, water runs off faster during the tropical rainy season, carrying away valuable topsoil. A World Bank study found that the rate of soil loss was 10 times higher on forest lands where slash-and-burn shifting cultivation was practiced than in undisturbed forests.

One reason that agricultural yields have fallen in sub Saharan Africa is that vast amounts of forest cover have disappeared, hastening soil erosion and loss of soil nutrients.

Forest cover regulates climate, while destruction of forests contribute to global warming. Whereas living trees soak up and store carbon dioxide from the atmosphere trees that are cut down and burned release carbon into the atmosphere. In the last decade tropical deforestation has released large amounts of stored carbon-accounting for roughly one-quarter of the carbon dioxide emissions to the atmosphere due to human activity.

Pressures on Forests

Current demand for forests products may exceed the limits of sustainable consumption by 25%. The developed world accounts for most of the demand for forest products. With just 16% of the world's population, North America, Europe, and Japan consume two-thirds of the world's paper and paperboard and half its industrial wood. Demand for industrial wood products also has risen in developing countries, however, along with demand for fuel wood, the main energy source for many rural communities.

Throughout the 1990s many developing countries with rapid population growth had high rates of deforestation. Forest land was converted to agricultural use, and trees cut to provide housing and wood for fuel. Moreover developing countries stepped up exports of forests, products to meet the rising demand from developed countries.

The amount of forest area per capita fell by half between 1960 and 1995—reflecting both population growth and the disappearance of forest cover. In 1995 close to 1.7 billion people lived in countries with less than one-tenth of a hectare of forest cover per capita (83). By 2025, an estimated 4.6 billion people will live in such countries.

What Can Be Done?

As population grows and per capita consumption of forest products increases, countries must do more to manage forest resources on a sustainable basis. The following developments offer encouragement:

Technological Improvements

Technological improvements including use of recycled paper and paperboard, have substantially reduced the amount of pulp needed to produce paper. In 1970 paper and paperboard consisted of 80% wood pulp. By 1997 more efficient production processes had reduced that figure to 56%. As a direct result, the production of pulp for paper is expected to grow by just over 1% a year over the next decade, about half the growth rate in the 1980s.

Forest Products Certification

Adopting a system that identifies forest products that come from sustainable managed forests could support efforts toward sustainability. As of 1998, about 10 million hectares of forest lands have been certified. Over 90% of the certified area is in northern, temperate forests, mostly in Europe and North America. Close to 60% of the entire certified area is in just two countries—Sweden and Poland—reflecting education and awareness campaigns in those countries. In tropical forests, where most of the destruction is taking place today, only tiny areas have been certified as providing sustainable yield.

Intergovernmental Responses

In 1995 the Intergovernmental Panel on forests (IPF) was established in response to the 1992 Earth Summit. The IPF evolved into the inter governmental Forum on Forests in 1997, after the UN's five-year review of the Earth Summit goals. The mission of the forum is to examine the underlying causes of deforestation and to help countries develop strategies that address them.

Efforts to advance an international legal convention on forests, which began in 1990, have been shelved, however. Some observes believe that advancing such a convention would only codify the standards of a weak consensus and thus would be worse than no convention at all. Widespread opposition to a convention makes it unlikely that the issues will reach the negotiating table.

Instead, many organizations urge governments of countries with large forest resources to enforce existing legislation and to introduce more effective forest conservation initiatives close to 130 countries have developed or updated their National Forest Programmes over the past decade.

While such initiatives are promising, they cannot be expected to halt forest destruction completely. Millions of people rely on forest products for their livelihoods. Sustainable forest management will require not just enforcement of laws that project forests but also alternative sources of livelihood for many rural people.

18

Population Growth and Natural Recreation Areas

Population growth during the past 50 years has made it difficult to set aside and conserve natural areas. Another half-century of growth will put even more pressure on protected areas as formerly small, distant settlements encroach on these sites and as the number of people (both local and visitors) who use these sites explodes.

National parks, forests, wildlife preserves, beaches, and other protected areas offer sanctuary to various habitats and indigenous communities, in addition to providing resources for local peoples. In an urbanizing world, these sites provide an opportunity for healthy interaction with the natural environment, as well as rare serenity.

From Buenos Aires to Bangkok, dramatic population growth in the world's major cities and the sprawl and pollution they bring-threatens natural recreation areas that lay beyond city limits. Tremendous growth in the population of Bombay has already engulfed Borivili National Park, a reserve that was beyond the city's periphery only a decade ago. With projected growth of 60 percent in the next 20 years, Bombay may soon swallow up more distant areas. On every continent, human encroachment has reduced both the size and the quality of natural recreation areas.

In nations where rapid population growth has outstripped the carrying capacity of local resources, protected areas become especially vulnerable. Although in industrial nations these areas are synonymous with camping, hiking, and picnics in the country, in Asia, Africa and Latin America most national parks, forests, and preserves are inhabited or used for natural resources by local populations.

An assessment by the World Conservation Union-IUCN of 30 protected sites in the developing world shows that these areas now act as magnets, attracting people to the rich oasis of water, fuel, food, and other resources they contain. Population growth rates in and around these areas are typically 2 percentage points above the national average-largely as a result of immigration from resource-starved areas.

As people seek out scarce resources, the resulting concentrations can be devastating. For example, population densities in the region surrounding Bwindi Impenetrable National Park in southern Uganda are some of the highest in all of Africa—exceeding 250 people for square kilometer. Though population at this site is expected to multiply, chronic land hunger already precipitates conflicts over fuel-wood collection, farming, cattle grazing, and bush burning.

Migration-driven population growth also endangers natural recreation areas in many industrial nations. Everglades National Park faces collapse as millions of new-comers move into South Florida.

Coastal recreation areas, including beaches, may be most burdened by the formidable combination of population growth and migration. All but one of the world's 15 largest cities-Mexico City—are coastal, and all of these cities will grow in the decades ahead. Whether it takes the form of expanding shantytowns in Kingston, Jamaica, or sprawling tract housing in southern California, virtually all the growth and movement in population in the next 50 years will occur in densely populated coastal corridors.

In nations already struggling to meet basic human needs, the prospect of establishing additional protected areas becomes increasingly slim. Throughout India, for example, while the national government designates areas as protected, state and local governments work to de-reserve these sites so that the resources can be harnessed to meet the needs of an additional 18 million Indians each year.

Sunbathers on beaches in Japan are often compared to sardines. People who use Central Park in New York City, which has nearly doubled in population since 1950, are faced with growing congestion and restrictions on activities. National parks throughout North America are confronted with huge backlogs of requests to visit, having to turn tourists away. Tourism at Yosemite has boomed from roughly 4,000 visitors in 1886 to more than 4 million people (and their cars) today. It is often remarked that "Americans love their national parks to death", as increased visitation degrades campsites, trails and wilderness.

Longer waiting lists and higher user fees for fewer secluded spots are likely the tip of the iceberg, as population growth threatens to eliminate the diversity of habitats and cultures, in addition to the peace and quiet, that protected areas currently house.

19

Myths and Illusions

The tide of precarity of rising steadily, so that people who have never been poor no longer regard poverty as a distant prospect but as one so close that it could engulf them at any moment.

In 1989, the fall of the Berlin Wall was rightly welcomed because it marked the collapse of a system that provided a degree of equality but rejected freedom. Today there is a strong possibility that the system gradually spreading all over the world—a kind of neo-liberal fundamentalism—may also collapse. In its obsession with freedom, vital though freedom is, this fundamentalism disregards equality, a term which should not be regarded here in purely static and statistical terms, but as something dynamic and ethical. Equality can only be truly practised in a context of social solidarity or to borrow from the vocabulary of the French Revolution of fraternity.

On the one hand, we have a world that is immensely rich in resources, possibilities, knowledge and experience; its constituent societies are freer and more dynamic than ever. There is an extraordinary potential for everyone to live a better life. But at the same time, new and ever higher walls are being built both between peoples and between social groups within individual countries. We are experiencing a travesty of development, which is creating a world bipolarized into extremes of wealth and poverty.

The most common reactions to this disastrous situation are very often the result of two misapprehensions. The first can only be described as ideological or doctrinaire since it is not based on the facts as they can be observed. It says that since the dominant system of values and things is by definition more than satisfactory, the persistence of impoverishment is merely a temporary blip. Enough time has elapsed, however, for us to see that this is not the case, including in countries where this system has been part of the established order for more than a century. One statistic is particularly eloquent. In jut over 30 years, world production has approximately doubled, but the gap has more than doubled between the income of the 20 per cent of world's people living in the richest countries and the income of the world's poorest 20 per cent, according to the United Nations Development Programme.

The second misapprehension stems from another form of blindness and illusion, namely the belief that poverty can be regarded exclusively as a moral issue, as if it had no other kind of implications for those who are not poor. Globalization is, however, a two-way process. It enable the countries of the North to export their values and their paradigms as well as their goods and capital to the countries of the South, but it also makes them much more vulnerable to the backlash of crises that afflict these countries. Even in the North, the cult of competitiveness is undermining situations once considered extremely stable. The tide of precarity is rising steadily, so that people who have never been poor no longer regard poverty as a distant prospect but as one so close that it could engulf them at any moment.

Because of inadequate socio-economic development, the extraordinary upsurge of democracy over the past 30 years remains a very fragile process, and there is a risk that the trend may be reversed. When hunger, disease and ignorance prevail, citizens' participation in decision-making becomes either non-existent or a mere charade. Democratic institutions become empty shells, representational bodies existing in form only and devoid of real significance.

Social divisions caused by economic distortions exacerbate the failures of democracy which in turn pose serious threats to civil order within countries and to peace between nations. It is high time to face these obvious facts.

20

Population and the Environment—The Global Challenge

As the century begins, natural resources are under increasing pressure, threatening public health and development. Water shortages, soil exhaustion, loss of forests, air and water pollution, and degradation of coastlines afflict many areas. As the world's population grows, improving living standards without destroying the environment is a global challenge.

Most developed economies currently consume resources much faster than they can regenerate. Most developing countries with rapid population growth face the urgent need to improve living standards. As we humans exploit nature to meet present needs, are we destroying resources needed for the future?

Environment Getting Worse

In the past decade in every environmental sector, conditions have either failed to improve, or they are worsening:

Public Health. Unclean water, along with poor sanitation, kills over 12 million people each year, most in developing countries. Air pollution kills nearly 3 million more. Heavy metals and other contaminants also cause widespread health problems.

Food supply. Will there be enough food to go around? In 64 of 105 developing countries studied by UN Food and Agricultural organisation, the population has been growing faster than food supplies. Population pressures have degraded some 2 billion hectares of arable land-an area the size of Canada and the US.

Fresh Water. The supply of freshwater is finite, but demand is soaring as population grows and use per capita rises. By 2025, when world population is projected to be 8 billion, 48 countries, containing 3 billion people will face shortages.

Coastlines and oceans. Half of all coastal ecosystems are pressured by high population densities and urban development. A tide of pollution is rising in the world's seas. Ocean fisheries are being overexploited, and fish catches are down.

Forests. Nearly half of the world's original forest cover has been lost, and each year another 16 million hectares are cut, bulldozed, or burned. Forests provide over US$400 billion to the world economy annually and are vital to maintaining healthy ecosystems. Yet, current demand for forest products may exceed the limit of sustainable consumption by 25%.

Biodiversity. The earth's biological diversity is crucial to the continued vitality of agriculture and medicine—and perhaps even to life on earth itself. Yet human activities are pushing many thousands of plant and animal species into extinction. Two of every three species is estimated to be in decline.

Global climate change. The earth's surface is warming due to greenhouse gas emissions, largely from burning fossil fuels. If the global temperature rises as projected, sea levels would rise by several meters, causing widespread flooding. Global warming also could cause droughts and disrupt agriculture.

Toward a Livable Future

How people preserve or abuse the environment could largely determine whether living standards improve or deteriorate. Growing human numbers, urban expansion, and resource exploitation do not bode well for the future. Without practicing sustainable development, humanity faces a deteriorating environment and may even invite ecological disaster.

Taking action. Many steps toward sustainability can be taken today. These include using energy more efficiently; managing cities better; phasing out subsidies that encourage waste; managing water resources and protecting freshwater sources; harvesting forest products rather than destroying forests; preserving arable land and increasing food production through a second Green Revolution; managing coastal ones and ocean fisheries; protecting biodiversity hotspots; and adopting an international convention on climate change.

Stabilizing population. While population growth has slowed, the absolute number of people continues to increase 0 by about 1 billion every 13 years. Slowing population growth would help improve living standards and would buy time to protect natural resources. In the long run, to sustain higher living standards world population size must stabilize.

21

Add Value, Go Global: Can Southern Firms Break into Export Markets?

The global economy has changed beyond recognition over the last decade. Widespread economic policy reform and in particular trade liberalisation have opened up new opportunities for developing countries. In poor countries, however, the consequences of trade liberalisation are not always positive. What can the private sector do to respond better and make the most of new trading opportunities? What factors have limited the impact of economic reforms on export performance?

Why have exports from poorer countries failed to increase more rapidly following trade liberalisation? What can be done to improve performance? Research on the response of firms in the private sector to economic reform can underpin new approaches to export promotion for poorer developing countries. For a long time, protective trade policies, poorly performing state-owned industries and state controls over the private sector were blamed for poor export performance in Africa and south Asia. Now that some of these problems have been remedied, other obstacles have come to light.

The effect of economic liberalisation and adjustment on the performance of poor countries has been cause for concern. Trade liberalisation should increase incentives to export and facilitate business enterprise by encouraging private ownership through privatisation and by attracting foreign investment. Macroeconomic stability ought to boost business confidence and performance. All these factors should promote exports, offsetting job and income losses caused by the closure or reorganisation of inefficient enterprises and industries yet, although some degree of reform and stability it is without export growth that was expected.

Trade reform and macroeconomic stability may be necessary conditions for improved export performance but by them are insufficient. The obstacles to improving export performance are numerous and there is no easy policy answer. The research programme examined export performance at three levels.

- Regional: how trade strategies should vary with skills and natural resource endowments
- National: factors influencing the export performance of manufacturing
- Sectoral: the performance of particular sectors of the economy.

The East Asian economies have shown that developing countries can complete successfully in global markets. For many, they provide a blueprint for economic growth applicable to many poor countries.

South Asia's comparative advantage lies in its abundant unskilled labour, while Africa's lies in its abundant natural resources. Different export promotion strategies are essential. South Asia's best prospectus are in labour-intensive manufacturing: the region's low level of exports would soar over the next decade if current obstacles to trade were reduced. Africa's exports could also increase but its biggest potential in primary products that need little educated labour and abundant natural resources.

Some African countries could also be substantial exporters of manufacturers, but their actual manufactured exports in most cases now fall far short. Comparing Ghana to Mauritius—one of Africa's most successful exporters of manufactured goods differences in firm—level efficiency are apparent Mauritian firms have more capital per worker and use it more efficiently. Reducing trade barriers is not sufficient. Wages in Ghana would have to be substantially lower to offset low labour productivity. Alternatively, labour productivity will have to be drastically improved if Ghanian firms are to compete successfully in export markets with wages at current levels.

Even when companies use capital and labour efficiently, poor infrastructure is a frequent stumbling products to export markets—an acute problem in landlocked countries and equally acute for manufacturers as research on Uganda clearly shows. What huts manufacturing exporters is being hit by the high cost of transporting their output to foreign markets and of transporting the materials they need from abroad. The cost penalties resulting from geography and poor infrastructure are far greater in Uganda than from high tariffs and other import restrictions.

Southern firms can still break into export markets, however. Developing-country firms do export to markets with exacting standards for product quality, reliability of delivery, and consumer safety. Two crucial aspects, however, are often overlooked:

- Non-manufacturing sectors, such as tourism and horticulture, generate significant employment and offer opportunities for supplying increasingly sophisticated products. Although manufacturing is considered more attractive, certain areas of tourism and horticulture can be equally appealing.
- New export opportunities are created are created as southern producers establish closer links with foreign customers. Producers of labour-intensive products such as garments, horticulture and footwear frequently depend on large retailers and specialist international traders for designs, information about demand and technical support.

Supermarkets make key decisions about which fruit and vegetables to grow, how they should be produced and processed and which firms should be included in the business. Strategic decisions by international producers and retailers in the footwear industry have been crucial in developing new production locations such as Vietnam and Romania. Similarly, work on automotive components production in South Africa and India illustrates how global sourcing by the leading motor companies closes off some markets and opens up others. Export prospects can only be evaluated in the light of global restructuring in these industries.

Emphasising global linkages does not mean that developing countries are powerless in the face of global forces. Even in tightly structured industries, there is scope for national policy and national strategy. Further more, there are important export sectors that are not structured in this way. Some tourism is dominated by large northern firms and is heavily import-dependent, but there is also enormous potential and national policy will be crucial in shaping the industry and its contribution to the economy as a whole.

For southern firms to break into export markets, certain issues must be addressed, especially in Africa. Some are recognised as important policy issues-investing in human capital and improving infrastructure for example. As one set of constraints are reduced—such as removing policy—induced distortions through trade liberalisation—another set takes precedence. In response to the integration of global markets, southern producers must join the global distribution chains to ensure markets for their exports.

These findings impose hard choices on developing countries. Should a firm allocate limited funds for investment in human capital or investment infrastructure? Future research might contribute by quantifying relative rates of return. On another level, countries may worry about the independence and autonomy of local producers if they are to join a global chain typically donated by northern companies. Rules regulate governmental trade and investment policies but who controls the global buyers and multinational companies whose decisions have such huge impacts on developing countries?

22

Employment and Promoting Ecology

How a Service Culture Could Put People back to Work

We are facing two big and urgent social problems: employment and ecology. Both the unemployment of millions of people and the progressive destruction of the ecosphere are alarming. But they are linked with each other. The 'greening' of industrial products, processes and services could provide many more jobs.

Unemployment has many causes, including:

- Sluggish Markets;
- Stagnating or declining purchasing power;
- Growing uncertainty about the future at all levels;
- Lack of will and/or ability to innovate.

But joblessness is by far due mostly to the high efficiency of industrial machinery, which produces ever more, ever faster, with ever fewer workers.

Waste or Resources

The extremely high productive use of human labour and the extremely low productive use of resources are manifested by gigantic mountains of waste. Already today, the junked cars on scrap heaps alone would form a line that would reach to the moon. The scene is the same with discarded electrical and electronic appliances. Every year, millions of tons of ovens, washing machines, refrigerators, dishwashers, TV sets, entertainment electronics equipment and small appliances are being wasted.

If we throw away all these things after a relatively short time we are not only being wasteful and irresponsible with resources, but equally so with people's work. For with the products and materials we discard, we also dispose of the human labour they contain. It is imperative that we radically reduce the enormous turnovers of material and energy. In other words, the productivity of raw materials and energy must be markedly increased. Specifically, that means we must draw as many services as possible from one kilogram of martial or 1 kWh of energy. Reducing the enormous flows of materials into the industrial system, as well as developing cycles of materials and responsibility (the manufacturer taken back and repairing and/or remanufacturing used products and materials) are the main pillars of a sustainable development that can cope with the future.

The industrialised nations must cut their consumption of raw materials by a factor of about 10 by 2050 if they are to be able to handle the challenges of the future. To achieve that reduction, innovation efforts must be directed at increasing resource productivity and/or ecological efficiency. In particular, strategies to extend the useful life of goods and intensify their use could result in reducing both the speed and volume of the flows of resources to industry.

Increasing Resource Productivity

In dealing with nature, we and industry are facing radical change. This is the transition from environmental protection (preservation of nature and health) to greater resource productivity (which at the same time means greater competitiveness). As a rule, environmental protection costs money, while higher resource productivity usually cuts manufacturing costs and/or increases a company's profitability. If the company can sell the same utility or benefits while using fewer resources, it saves twofold: in buying raw materials and on waste disposal. Thereby the rule is that goods and components cycles are more profitable than resources cycles, and that the company which is first in the market gains an additional compotitive advantage in terms of a lead in knowledge and image. If a service, or benefits in the form of services, can be sold instead of products, the decoupling of company success and materials flows is even greater.

Impacts on Employment

The two social problem areas of work and ecology have to date been perceived and treated separately in politics, in industry and in our own minds. And, I believe, with little result. The link between the two must be established.

The strategies to boost resource productivity would have considerable impacts on the change in industrial structures, on handling existing product inventories, and on employment. In particular, the strategies would lead to a switch of focal point from a raw materials-intensive and use-value-related service economy. This is where another view of profitability comes in. Business management would no longer focus on value added, but on maintenance of value over longer periods based on the intrinsic value of a product. Expressed as a question, the value factor, which would move to the centre of business thinking and dealing, means: how can the utilisation value be improve and sold? How can products be made with as few raw materials and as little energy as possible and create a high benefit as pollutant-free as possible for as long as possible during their entire life-cycle?

With regard to employment, the production of long-life goods would appear at first sight to lead to a reduction in the need for work. In fact, however, the strategies to increase resource productivity have positive net employment impacts. The reason is that saving resources is based in principle on substituting energy by work, rather than the reverse as has been customary to date.

If the useful life of products is extended, that will not only preserve most of the materials and energy they contain as well as the work invested in them. The products will also require a considerable amount of mostly skilled work input. Reconditioning products is as a rule more labour-intensive than manufacturing them. So large-scale reconditioning and repair work increase the number of skilled jobs and at the same time reduces the inflows of materials and energy.

Comparing a car with a life-cycle of 20 years with two others that each have useful lives of 10 years gives a good example. The first car causes an increase in employment per life-year of about 50 per cent in terms of total work input in manufacture, service, repairs and reconditioning while at the same time reducing the energy consumption by half.

Regionalisation of Industry

Extending product service life would also mean replacing energy and/or capital by skilled work, helping to save money to boot. But not only rising costs of disposal, materials and energy would reduce consumption. Increasing transport costs would also mean that carrying all kinds of freight halfway around the world would make less and less business sense. That would result in ever more products and materials being circulated, reconditioned, and recycled or reduced on a regional basis. In turn, that would create regional jobs, and be more profitable as well as more promotive of technology-not only from ecological aspects.

In addition, a way of doing business which encompassed material and responsibility cycles would no longer differentiate between manufacturing and reconditioning, or between marketing and remarketing. The structure of such as economy would be predominantly decentralised and regionalised so that it could adapt itself to the new cycles. It also would benefit from the greater efficiency of the new working practices.

True, jobs would be lost in the sectors of central production, and raw materials extraction and processing. But at the same time, more and higher-skilled jobs would emerge. These would not only be better qualified jobs, but also decentralised because reconditioning, repairs and maintenance must be done near the customer. And that, in turn, would also reduce goods traffic.

In addition, skilled workers would be needed because in many cases of small production runs it makes sense and is also more economical to hire such people. They can work faster and more flexibly-and mostly cheaper than fully automated production lines.

There also would be a growing need for maintenance, repairs and reconditioning. More and more people would be wanted for reconditioning, that is, the remanufacturing of old products. As reconditioning involves far more craft work than highly rationalised new production, there would be a positive impact on the labour market if there were more of the former and correspondingly less of the latter.

From Production to Services

Switching to long-life products and changing from selling products to selling use-values would strengthen the current trend of jobs shifting from industrial production to the service sector. For example, if the service of individual transport were to be sold instead of the product car, the company with the competitive advantage would be the one that had a service centre in every town and village, with appropriately staffed workshops and sales or rental facilities.

Enduring change towards a knowledge-intensive and use-value-related service economy would not only mean that more people would be needed to fill jobs. It would offer more opportunities for part-time work, as well as possibilities of employment for older people and the handicapped. People who earlier could not keep up with the pace of working life would be more inclined to return to it. Another impact would be that many companies would reduce their dependence on the world market. They would no longer switch certain tasks abroad, but assign them to their part-time employees, helping them to meet their commitments as self-employed entrepreneurs.

The latter would be accommodated by an ecology-driven fiscal reform which would make massive cuts or changes in subsidies and raise the cost of energy and raw materials consumption. This move would be accompanied by a reduction in income tax and non-wage costs such as social security contributions. The market would thus be more efficient, energy—and material—intensive new production more expensive, labour-intensive repair work and reconditioning cheaper, and jobs would remain in the home country or region.

A number of more recent studies show clearly that an ecological tax reform would help to create jobs, and thereby could make a decisive contribution to reducing unemployment.

23

Heating up Environmental Education and Communication

Worldwide environmental issues ranging from the hazardous waste in your backyard to ozone depletion far away in the atmosphere can threaten our planet and compromise our quality of life. The positive and negative effects of environmental interactions are just beginning to be better understood and addressed. Within this context, environmental education and communication have a remarkable opportunity to accelerate understanding and to mobilize national and community participation in change.

Communication because it is the exchange of information. In social programmes, its effectiveness depends on assessing audience needs and taking into account the social, cultural and economic aspects of a problem as well as the quality of education messages and materials.

Education because it involves learning—learning how to think about an issue and its solution; how to acquire and refine skills for solving problems; how to transfer what is learned from situation to situation.

In social programmes, communication and education together lead to increased public participation in problem-solving and in activities which promote change. The participation of many individuals over time can lead to changed expectations for individual behaviour and institutional practices.

The process of communication and education together might be thought of as the "heating up" of a society around an issue through the "saturation" of all available channels of communication. In a "hot" society, all channels of communication and the processes of individual and social change reinforce a message. From the perspective of designing an education and communication programme, this might be called the "saturation" approach to social change.

Example of 'Saturation'

A decade ago, research information about the link between smoking and chronic disease, particularly cancer and heart attack, was communicated to health professionals in a hostile environment where smoking was considered socially "in". But information campaigns by governments and cancer/heart associations put smoking on the public agenda. The result? Conversations about smoking increased within households, doctors' offices and in laboratories. Community organizations began to take action. Schools and the work place joined in.

No-smoking campaigns became a catalyst for change in attitudes and behaviour in health with "smoking" as an unifying symbol. Under the umbrella of "smoking", the rituals and behaviours associated with smoking were individually affected by the saturation process. Therefore other health activities related to smoking also reaped the benefits. Extending the impact of saturation can be applied to other contexts.

Today, a new global image is emerging—an image which represents the environment and unifies people behind its common cause. The symbol of a "Green" earth and the colour "green" are perpetuating an environmental movement, the result of and an inspiration to environmental education and communication efforts everywhere.

"Green" political parties are gaining popular support. All over the world "green" label marketing approaches are influencing consumer behaviour. Just as in the smoking example, acting upon the unifying symbol of "green" through environmental education and communication has the potential to strengthen programmes and further heat up public consciousness. Environmental education and communication provides the opportunity to support policy change, institutional change and behaviour change in highly segmented audiences.

Stage 1: Setting the Public Agenda

Globally, the public is already talking about the environment. Numerous single-issue environmental groups and educational programmes are already in operation. People become ready to talk about, think about and support environmental activities. Membership in existing environmental groups increases, and new programmes and opportunities for popular participation appear.

Stage 2: Engaging Key Institutions

Building alliances and collaboration among institutions creates a network. Lead institutions reach out to other institutions representing social process—education, work, religion and government—and initiate collaborative educational activities. For example, school systems integrate environmental modules within existing curricula and initiate teacher training and youth ecoclubs. Community based action increasingly addresses local issues such as garbage collection and industrial pollutants. Media coverage responds more frequently and positively.

Stage 3: Establishing a New Environmental Order

Governmental and non-governmental institutions become the initiators of environmental education, and participation becomes broader and more diverse. Specific target audiences begin to modify their role with regard to particular environmental problems. Community mobilization increasingly generates demand for appropriate regulatory change. Expectations for appropriate individual and social behaviour begin to change. Finally, "Green" positions become "in", "non-Green" positions "out".

Applied Research

Experience with development communication in other sectors leads to optimism in reaching new levels of excellence in combining environmental education and communication. Perhaps the most important element in "putting it all together", however, is to maintain commitment to well-tried applied research procedures.

- Investigation of target audience characteristics (including socio-economic, gender and cultural) and attributes (attitudinal and behavioural) in relation to local environmental issues provides insight into an appropriate model of behaviour change and effective educational strategies, messages and materials.
- Limited testing of innovative strategies devised for local situations will uncover refinements needed for broader application.
- Comparision studies between the impact of different educational strategies with similar objectives will provide a basis for future strategic choices.
- Standardized indicators of impact and evaluation studies will provide an assessment of the progress and impact of programmes and, to some extent, the relative power of different components within the programmes.
- Content analyses of mass media over time will provide profiles of societies "heating up" on environmental issues.
- Description of the differences between industrialized country and developing country objectives, programme content and impact will provide a source of new insight about the process of social and individual change.

In addition, applied research can also advance the state of the art for environmental education and communication when properly field tested. There are two major sources for such innovation:

1. the refinement of social change theory at universities and research firms:
2. "creative" concepts with proved efficacy in other sectors such as the "enter-educate" approach (education through entertainment) in the populations sector.

This description of the potential and progress of environmental education and communication is, in reality, a call to action. The "heating up" of societies on environmental issues is technically within our reach through environmental education and communication programmes. It is up to us to develop the funding, the research-based strategies—and the communication among professionals about results, both successes and failure—required to make it happen.

24

Money Alone is Not Enough

Technology Transfer and Environmental Protection

In the seventies it was a hotly debated topic, in the eighties it became a moot issue: The demand of the developing countries for low-cost or even free technology transfers from the industrial nations. The environment, or more accurately, the endangered environment, is responsible for reviving this subject once believed to be dead. Politicians in the South were quick to see the opportunity which presented itself: No environmental protection without technology, no technology without technology transfer, not technology transfer without money.

The Montreal treaty (on the reduction of chlorofluorocarbon production) was an important first step. It established a fund which supports the environmental efforts of the developing countries. But this was only the beginning. Technology was one of the main concerns of the Untied Nations conference on Environment and Development (UNCED).

It is undisputed that private enterprises control the expertise necessary for environmentally sound technologies. The discussions in the developing countries revolve around this basic issue: What guarantees are there that these firms will transfer any technologies at all and at an acceptable price to boot? Both premises present a problem: In all likelihood, technology monopolists have invested substantial amounts in the development of the respective technology and will therefore try to sell their licenses at the highest possible price

(price problem). Having had so many failures with specific projects in the past, many firms are not quite reluctant to transfer technology to the developing countries. It was no coincidence that North-South technology transfers practically came to a standstill in the eighties.

Technology cannot be purchased as a package. This is a frequently forgotten truism. By general definition, technology consists of four components:

- Hardware, for instance a specific configuration of machines and equipment to manufacture a product or provide a service.
- Know-how, i.e. scientific and technical knowledge, qualifications, and empirical knowledge;
- Organization, i.e. the arrangement which combines hardware, know-how, and operational management methods;
- The end product, i.e. the item or service.

The technical components (machines, blueprints) and products (licenses) can be purchased subject to the cited restrictions, but not organization and qualifications. This is the real bottleneck for technological development in most developing countries. There is not inducive to the process which is most important for the utilization of technology technological learning.

The core of technological knowledge is the mastery and subsequent continuous improvement of production processes. In part this happens automatically (learning by doing), but beyond that it must be actively stimulated. Many examples in both industrial and developing countries show that firms frequently stagnate at a certain technological level, thus missing a chance to improve efficiency. The main reason is inadequate technological knowledge. The secret of optimizing the conversion process lies in a strategy of small steps, the steady improvement of individual segments.

The economically most dynamic developing countries are successful because of high productivity increases made possible by technological competence, i.e. the ability to assess and evaluate the technology offer, to select, utilize, and improve technologies, and ultimately develop new ones. This latest state-of-the at processes can be used for industrial expansion projects. As far as these countries are concerned, the introduction of financing mechanisms for the transfer of environmentally sound technologies represents a very promising approach.

Technological Competence the Crucial Factor

In other countries industrialization efforts have caused serious environmental degradation but little economic development. The reason is last but no least inadequate, only slowly growing technological competence. Those countries have hardly any money to invest in environmentally sound technologies. But even if the international community establishes financing mechanism, the problem of inadequate technological competence remains unsolved. It is unreasonable to assume that in a country, where conventional production technologies are used ineffectively and inefficiently, environmentally sound technologies can suddenly be applied in a meaningful and efficient manner. For these countries the transfer of environmentally sound technologies is a "quick fix" which in all likelihood will not work. Without an established level of national technological competence, it will not do much good to shower a country with technology from outside (more precisely, with technical hardware and production know-how).

This brings us to an original development policy problem. Technology and technology transfer have always played a big role in development policy, although quite often the perspective was short-term: Instead of technology, only hardware was transferred; frequently, technological competence was not developed in the recipient countries, but rather substituted with external experts. In the future, much more emphasis will have to be placed on stimulating the technological learning process and promoting national technological competence. Many developing countries have already moved in this direction, such as instituting macro-political reforms, which pressure private industry to increase performance, thus forcing technological learning. But development policy can make a contribution as well. Above all, it will have to adopt a more systemic approach and promote structural improvements at several levels:

- As a systemic link between project and project environment. Technology institutions have always been the darling of environmental policy, but frequently they had too little contact with potential users and therefore remained ineffective.
- As linkage with indigenous efforts in the recipient countries and with the activities of other donors. Isolated projects and competition among donors are a guarantee for failure. On the other hand, the fascination in many recipient countries with individual technologies is slowly being replaced by a growing understanding of the technological correlations, concerted technological-political actions, which have already been initiated in some developing countries (for instance Thailand, Jordan and Tanzania) and which brought together representatives of government, private industry, educational and research institutions at "round table" discussions, provide an opportunity for the systemic incorporation of technologically oriented development policy measures.

A Dual Challenge for the Industrial Nations

The industrial nations are thus faced with a dual challenge. First, they must support those developing countries financially whose technological competence is adequate for the effective utilization of environmentally sound technologies. On a global scale, this is an ecologically rewarding undertaking. Since environmental standards have been low in these countries, investments can achieve substantially higher reductions of pollutants than in the industrialized North. There is another aspect: The industrial nations can put pressure on the developing countries to use environmentally sound processes only if they simultaneously offer financial compensation. Secondly, the industrial nations must increase their efforts to raise the level of technological competence in developing countries. This is an essential pre-condition for the developing countries to be able to participate in the medium term in an environmentally benign growth model.

25

World Trade—The Next Challenge

On 15 December 1993 the world changed. May be not as dramatically as the moment when the Berlin Wall fell, but then unlike that very necessary demolition job, the success of the Uruguay Round was a work of construction. Like the destruction of the wall, though, its effects will be profound and lasting ones felt far beyond its immediate context. It will be seen as a defining moment in modern history.

The importance of the Round can be seen in terms of boost it gives to job creation; to development; to investment; to economic reform; to the rule of law and in many other ways besides. All of these benefits are real and important. But the true value of the whole is much, much more than the sum of these parts.

Put simply, governments came to the conclusion that the notion of a new world order was not merely attractive but absolutely vital; that the reality of the global market—whatever ambitions some of them may retain for regional tegration—required a level of multilateral cooperation never before attempted.

No Losers in the Round

It has created a revolutionary framework for economic, legal and political cooperation. But now turn to the immediate results of the Round. Seeing them as a profit and loss account or a scorecard of winners and losers is to see them in static terms, as one-off conclusions with finite effects. This misses the point completely.

Every nation now needs an effective trading system, but especially so the small and poor. They have it. Everyone will also gain from the huge package of market access results even if they did not get every concession they were seeking from trading partners—it is the biggest market access deal ever negotiated.

However, the essence of the Uruguay Round's achievements is that they are dynamic. The new agreements, the new rules and structures it sets up—all mean a commitment to a continuing process of cooperation and reform of which the agreement in December was only the beginning.

Maintaining the liberalizing momentum will call for continuing effort and vigilance by participating countries. But now their energy can be focused through the Round's greatest innovation; the new World Trade Organisation (WTO) in place of the improvised basis on which the GATT has operated for 45 years, trade will now have a permanent forum appropriate to its importance in the world economy.

Technically speaking, the WTO will oversee the implementation of the Round's results, administer all the agreements in goods, services and intellectual property, and manage the unified dispute settlement system. But beyond these administrative functions, it will raise the political profile of trade a profile which has already been lifted greatly by the Uruguay Round. The WTO will have regular instead of occasional–direct ministerial involvement. It will have a clear mandate to act as a forum for further trade negotiations. Most of all it will complete the transition from a trading system which largely restricted itself to policies at the border to one which also covers most aspects of domestic policy-making affecting international competition in goods and services, as well as investment.

Through the WTO, the Round will change the way the world economy is shaped. But it is not the final victory over protectionism and unilateralism. Any premature rejoicing would have quickly been cut short by the evidence since 15 December that major economic powers are still ready to take the unilateral approach to trade problems. Arguments for protectionism based on the alleged threat of low-cost competition to production and jobs will not just fade away because the Round is a success. The seductive appeal of "beggar-thy-neighbour" policies is highlighted by the seemingly greater vigour of the lobbies for protectionism than the advocates of open markets.

These dangers—and the speech with which they have resurfaced—make the achievement of the Uruguay Round all the more important, and its successful implementation all the more urgent. Implementation requires more than mutual backslapping about what we have achieved. It requires now that the US, EU and Japan, in particular, rapidly obtain final authority to ratify and also take a lead in providing the WTO with the means to fulfil its mandate.

The success of the Round has come at a time when it is even more vitally needed than anyone could have guessed when it was launched in 1986. Old structures and alignments have been turned inside out in trade as in every other area of international relations. We face a world of change and challenge, in which the reinforced trading system will be a primary source of stability and security.

The developing countries including India have become enthusiastic supporters of the multilateral trading system and the Uruguay Round even if all their demands were not met by industrial countries. The reasons lie in the changing economic policies of many developing countries and the clearer appreciation of the value of the GATT system that has grown along with these changes.

The challenge of new issues in world trade will be a major one for the WTO. The new organization has to consider issues such as the links between trade and the environment, international competition policy, trade and investment, and trade and labour standards. To say a few words about trade and the environment since it is one area in which GATT member countries have committed themselves already to a comprehensive new work programme. They decided on 15

December, in conjunction with the adoption of the results of the Uruguay Round negotiations, to draw up a work programme on trade and environment by the Ministerial meeting in Marrakesh. Environmental policy-making is one of the most rapidly evolving areas of national and international policy-making, and it is entirely appropriate that emphasis should be placed now in GATT/WTO on ensuring better policy coordination and multilateral cooperation over the linkages between trade and environment.

Permanent Negotiations

The Uruguay Round may well be the last of its kind, but this in no way means the end of multilateral trade negotiations. On the contrary, it means they become a permanent event. Adhoc negotiating rounds were necessary mainly because the GATT lacked the mandate or the institutional basis to operate the multilateral system to the full on a continuous basis. Between rounds the GATT has tended to lose momentum, often at the very times when it was essential to make the most of the liberalizing impulse. This has allowed protectionism and unilateralism to recover and regroup and meant that each round has to start by regaining lost ground.

The positive results of the Uruguay Round will redefine much more than assumptions about trade. If they are exploited with the same determination, courage and commitment that went into concluding the Round, they should mean nothing less than a new start for sustainable growth and a new system of collective economic security for the world.

But if the trading system is now up to the job of supporting multilateral cooperation on such a wide scale, do the other structures of economic cooperation still meet the bill? The establishment of the WTO will put trade and investment on a par—perhaps rather in advance—of cooperation in monetary and financial areas. The WTO will stand alongside its original Bretton Woods sisters, the IMF and the World Bank. The three institutions must learn to work together even more effectively and closely. For example, rather than each body conducting separate reviews of country policies, is there not a case to be made for a more integrated approach on country reviews? But that does not, on its own, add up to effective multilateral economic cooperation. The question really has to be asked seriously: are the G7, the OECD, the regional groupings adequate to provide that cooperation?

It is the next challenge of international economic leadership—the challenge of translating the common interest in global growth into a practical and effective mechanism for solving our common economic problems together. So, the Ministers meeting in Marrakesh is an historic event which will establish the World Trade Organization and put in place the new multilateral trading system, they will be making not an end, but a beginning.

26

Migration

The scale and diversity of today's migrations are beyond any previous experience. Rapid urban growth and environmental degradation in rural areas have led to internal migration affecting hundreds of millions of people. Migration is now seen as a priority issue equal in political weight to other major global challenges such as the environment, population growth and economic imbalances between regions.

Families and households form the basis for economic growth, social development and personal fulfillment. Decisions, by individual women and men on marriage, family, a place to live, shape the destinies of communities and nations. National policies and international conditions provide the context for individual decision-making. Effective development policies, including population, reproductive health and family planning policies, address this reality.

Data on national and global population trends set the agenda for national policy. An important element of population programmes is gathering data that will allow policy-making responsive to the realities of daily life, and to the needs and aspirations of individuals.

The dominant feature of global demographics is still growth. Age distribution is a growing concern, as the numbers of young and elderly people, grow, relative to the working-age population. The world is growing steadily more urban. From being a sign of strength and dynamism in the national economy, the rate and scale of urban growth has become increasingly a cause for concern. The influx of migrants to the biggest cities may be weakening both urban and rural sectors.

International migration is small in extent compared with internal movements, but has a disproportionate impact. Both internal and international migration are driven by population growth, and by inequities between countries. Migration is one of the choices which shape people's lives and the destiny of nations. But it can also be a symptom of inequity and underdevelopment. Migrants are by definition the most vulnerable members of the host community. Their living and working conditions should be protected.

Open and frank exchange of information and views between host and sending countries is needed more than ever. The aim of the international community should be to protect the right to move, but to ensure that movement is voluntary and that it stimulates rather than holds back personal and national development. "The point of departure should be the human right to live and work where one pleases, so long as it does not infringe on other people's rights to do the same."

The Urban Transformation

The rural sector is declining in importance and its contribution to national economies. It is increasingly part of unified economy based on the city. Contact with the urban areas is easier than ever and is encouraged by rural development.

Temporary and circular migration is giving way to more permanent settlement. The largest cities are under increasing strain, and residents and encountering increasing difficulties in improving or even maintaining living conditions. Nevertheless, migration continues, driven by a variety of forces both positive and negative. The choice to move can be part of a strategy for survival or personal development; but it is often enforced by external conditions.

The urban transformation is irreversible, but the rural sectors must also be strengthened to balance the developing economy. Attention to gender issues will be crucial in ensuring a successful transition. The forces driving internal and international migration have much in common. Demographic pressures are contributing to both. As the pressures encouraging migration increase, the options for migrants become more limited. This collision is contributing to the atmosphere of crisis surrounding both urban and international migration.

Costs and Benefits

Migration is the result of individual or family decisions. But it is also part of social processes. In economic terms, migration is as much a global phenomenon as trade in commodities or manufactured goods. It is part of a broader pattern, and evidence of changing economic, social and cultural relationships.

But migration may be evidence of a different kind of relationship: the combination of poverty, rapid population growth and environmental damage is a powerful destabilizing factor driving urban growth and eventually international migration. On the recipient side, migration has usually been seen as evidence of a thriving economy: today's industrial states were built in part by migrant labour, skills and investment. In today's increasingly uncertain conditions, migration may be seen as a threat to the security and well-being of the local workforce and society at large.

The only effective means to reduce migration pressures over the long term are to slow population growth; to stimulate economic growth and job creation at home, and promote the development of the individual and the family as the basic economic and social unit.

A Question of Gender

It is often assumed that most migrants are men, in reality, women make up nearly half of the international migrant population. Gender differences in social and economic roles affect migration decision making, household strategy, and the sex composition of labour migration. Attention to the gender dimension of migratory movements ought to be an important component in population and development planning.

Women frequently take the initiative in migration decisions, which may reflect limited opportunities in rural areas. Low status limits women's choices at home and may increase pressure to migrate, but it may also affect life in the host community. Opportunities may be limited by lack of education or skills, or by customer limitation on women's freedom of action outside the family or ethnic group. Paid employment for migrant women is usually in the lowest wage, least secure, and lost status jobs, mostly in housework, child care and trade.

Most educated women end up in the same low-status, low-wage production and service jobs as unskilled female migrants. Men, too, experience downward mobility, but the contrast in the decline in women's employment status is far greater. Despite these disadvantages women migrants have become significant economic actors. Their status may be improved by migration, but the advantages are not clear-cut. Women's status as migrants is affected by their vulnerability, and by their lack of reproductive freedom. To ensure improved status they will need both legal protection and essential services, including reproductive health services.

Refugees

Refugees in the 1990s are overwhelmingly in Asia, and Latin America. Their numbers are large, about 17 million, and growing rapidly. A further 3.5 to 4 million were thought to be in "refugee-like situations", though estimates are probably extremely conservative, and an estimated 23 million people internally displaced.

It is important to recognize the common roots of refugee and other forms of mass movement of populations. At the same time, despite the difficulty of distinguishing between political and socio-economic causes of migration, there is a clear need to distinguish between refugees and other groups of migrants. Participation in international efforts of burden-sharing would ensure that most refugee problems would be dealt with in their regions of origin.

Conclusions and Policies

Migration highlights linkages and interdependencies within countries, with many implications for development agendas, including population programmes and development assistance.

Policies to regulate or moderate international migration have concentrated largely on urban growth. They have been only intermittently effective. The most successful have concentrated on stimulating rural development and the growth of alternative urban centers.

Migration is also a personal or family decision, which is affected by external conditions such as poverty or environmental degradation, improving conditions of personal and family life can make a crucial difference in the decision to migrate, reducing dependence on migration as a strategy. Because migrations the result of personal and family decisions, it can be influenced by policies that improve the quality of life.

This offers the opportunity for policies emphasizing individual development, among them education, health (including reproductive health) and family planning. Such policies are particularly relevant to the Strategies must take into account gender differences in social and economic life and the differential effects of policies.

Migration decisions are about family security and long-term-life-chances, rather than simply the maximization of income. They are ultimately strategies designed to look after the individual's and the house-hold's needs, safeguard their security, and respond to their aspirations. If the goal is to reduce migration pressures through development it will be essential to increase the capacity but reduce the need to migrate. Long-term external support will be required to make such policies a reality, particularly in areas of rapid population growth and potential mass outward flows. Highly coordinated allocation of development assistance can help establish priorities and focus attention on basic needs. The challenge to both international donors and co-operating governments is to direct programme spending to the areas where it can be most effective.

27

Living with Diversity

Fishers' nets and loggers' saws may directly impoverish local ecosystems, but most biological losses have root causes far away, in long-settled urban areas and farms where diversity is seldom a concern, but where steadily rising demand for food, water, wood and other resource—and the dispersal of resulting wastes—reach far beyond the settled areas themselves. In general, these peopled landscapes have lost much of their own biological wealth, but what remains is still important to their continued functioning and livability. Reconciling farms and cities with diversity will require stopping the damage they bring to remaining natural habitats, but also beginning to halt and reverse the homogenization of these unnatural habitats.

Uniformity is not inherently undesirable. In fact, to some degree, homogeneity is the basis of all agriculture: a given type of plant is favored and others are suppressed or eliminated. But trends in recent decades (most notably the Green Revolution and the parallel intensification of farming systems in industrial nations) have pushed uniformity to dangerous levels.

The unsustainability of modern agriculture is in part a measure of its inability to tolerate diversity. Both genetic and ecological uniformity—the sameness of fields sown horizon to horizon without interruption—demand costly and often futile reliance on chemicals to protect crops from pests or diseases that are rapidly spreading and evolving. The drive the leave no hectare unplowed worsens soil erosion, pushing tractors onto highly erodible hillsides and removing windbreaks, hedgerows and other remnant habitats.

Some of agriculture's biological impacts are obvious—the expansion of arms onto forests and wetlands, for example. While the increasing reliance on chemical inputs and machinery has reduced these impacts in some cases by decreasing the area needed to produce a given amount of food, it has worsened others.

A fundamental transition away from today's wasteful and polluting farming systems is needed to put the world's food supplies on a secure footing. Many of the reforms that will reduce farming's dependence on fossil fuel inputs and its misuse of soils and waters can also restore diversity to agricultural landscapes. Pesticides, for example, kill not only pests but other animals, such as pollinators and predators, that are beneficial to agriculture. Alternative pest control measure that lower pesticide use can also, ironically, reduce pest damage to crops by reviving the diversity of soil and insect communities, which play crucial roles in maintaining soil productivity and checking the spread of pest outbreaks.

Traditional agroecosystems are important not only because they provide sustenance to rural people and harbor valuable genetic resources, but also because they contain the seeds of a sustainable, diversity-based mode of agriculture. At varying levels, diversity is the basis of production for many peasants. Farmers often mix strains of a given crop in their fields as a hedge against the vagaries of weather. They also tend to recognize the dependence of their farms on adjacent ecological systems and to tolerate wild plants (often crop relatives whose continued interbreeding with domestic descendants contributes to genetic variety) on the outskirts of their fields.

Population growth and the expansion of large commercial farms have rendered many once-sound practices no longer viable, and traditional agriculture badly needs infusions of money and research to increase its modest yields without abandoning its stability.

Urban areas, with good reason, are considered the antithesis of natural diversity. Only the most resilient creatures (many of them regarded as weeds and pests) thrive in them, and cities' ceaseless expansion, consumption of resources, and emissions of waste threaten both farmland and wilderness almost everywhere. As with agricultural lands, the first priority for urban areas is to half their expansion onto other ecosystems and reduce the damage they export, such as the sewage poured onto coral reefs by burgeoning coastal cities throughout the tropics, or the wasteful consumption of tropical hardwoods in Japanese building construction.

But even concrete jungles can support some diversity. Landscaping of private yards and public spaces with native vegetation can not only reduce the expense and environmental impact of watering, spraying and hauling the remains of sterile grass monocultures, but also help revive bird and other wildlife populations. Most urban areas also have water-ways running through them, or corridors of unused land such as steep ravines; if their use as waste receptacles is reduced, these can be maintained or restored as wildlife habitat.

In developing nations, especially, a surprising amount of agricultural production takes place within city limits, in home gardens. These hidden farmlands contain a great deal of genetic diversity, and their expansion could help reduce the scale and environmental impacts of commercial agriculture.

One reason that the destruction of biological diversity has gone so far without major public commitments to stopping it is that urban dwellers have little experience of the natural and even less understanding of its importance. Restoring nature where people live—reestablishing a personal link with the living world—may be necessary to save it elsewhere. For all the rational arguments favoring long-term protection of biological assets, people who have lost all direct sense of their dependence on natural systems may simply not care.

Only a growing respect for diversity for its own sake—beginning, perhaps, with a reconnection between people and nature within the urban environment—will trigger altruistic responses among those wealthy enough to have the option of considering the needs of future generations and natural communities. Although many conservation measures make economic sense, arguments of economics or self-interest will likely fail to be convincing when the contest is between a few uncharismatic species of unknown value and a major industrial projects. "Human beings make sacrifies for what they love." Those who maintain strong bonds with the biological world on which they depend may be more inclined to make the hard decisions needed to protect it.

28

Cheap Transport for India's Millions

Cities congested with cars and buses. Trucks overloaded with goods and passengers. Trains with people clinging to doors and windows in a desperate attempt to get into the crammed interior. These are images of transport in Third World countries which can be observed almost everywhere. Transport is growing at an unprecedented rate: through population growth, through increased mobility of people and the evergrowing trade within and among nations. In most countries, even in the industrialized world, infrastructure is barely able to keep pace with the growth in demand for transportation. Cheap, efficient and environmentally safe transport systems are needed for the movement of people and goods. India, is one of the few developing countries with a well functioning mass transportation system. With the exception of China, no other developing country can boast of a comparable railway network.

140 years of Railway History

Indian Railways are seen by many as a unifying factor in a country which is made up of many different ethnic, cultural and religious groups. Its origions go back to the middle of the last century. The first line was opened in 1853 on a 34 kilometer stretch between Boribunder and Thana near Borribay. In the following year, the first stretch of the Calcutta to Delhi line was opened. Within half a century, a railway system came into being which not only linked the major production centers with the seaports on the Indian Ocean but also crisscrossed the mountainous center of India with its steep mountain ridges, the Western and Eastern Ghats. When India achieved independence from Britain in 1947, most of the present railway network was already in place.

The railways were built by the British not only in order to facilitate internal and external trade, but also for military and strategic reasons in order to be able to rush troops to the borders to protect the Empire or to quell internal unrest. Another reason for creating a mass transport system were the frequent famines which could only be conquered if it was possible to rapidly transport large amounts of food from surplus to deficit areas. The railways thus became an instrument for internal development—contrary to the situation in many African colonies of the time where railways were built with the sole objective of carrying export produce and minerals to the nearest port.

An impediment to efficiency of the Indian Railways was the fact, though, that construction was not planned and implemented by a central authority but by a great number of private companies and governments of India's states. In 1948, when a major effort was made to bring the railways under central control, there were as many as 42 independent railway systems, some very big, some serving only a tiny principality in the central highlands. The situation after independence was made worse through the partition of the former British India into two separate states which disrupted the railway network as it had evolved in the 19th and 20th centuries. In 1951-52, the government regrouped the entire rail network into six railway zones which were later split up further to form the presently existing nine zones. The amalgamation of the railways under one central administration with nine regional centers was the precondition for the necessary standardization of the permanent way, bridges, rolling stock, and equipment.

Standardization was and is a problem for the Indian Railway even more than 47 years after independence. A costly legacy left by the British railway designers are the three different gauges on which trains are running to this day:

broad gauge, meter gauge and narrow gauge. Modernization efforts by the railway administration are now concentrated on gradually converting the whole network to broad gauge.

Impressive Achievements

In view of the difficulties faced by the Indian Railways at independence, its development since those days is impressive: in 1950-51, 73 million tons of freight and 1.284 million passengers were carried; these figures rose to 318 million tonnes of freight and 3.858 million passengers in the year 1992-93. These gains were almost entirely achieved through an increase in efficiency. The rail network grew only slightly at a rate of 1.3 per cent per year.

Modernization also applies to track renewal and electrification of railway lines. Steam engines which are still in use in some parts of the country will be phased out until the turn of the century. The emphasis is on creasing the speed of passenger and freight trains to enlarge the capacity of the existing railway network.

A problem for the modernization programme is the dwindling financial support of the railways through the Indian Government. Whereas allocations for the railways reached a peak of 15.45 per cent of the total budget in the mid-sixties, the share of the railways is now down to 3.4 per cent. The shortfall in investment funds which the railways need to push through their ambitious modernization programme could be made up by mobilizing their own resources if the Railways had the freedom to do their own pricing of services. This, however, is not possible. A large part of the freight such as foodgrains and fertilizers has to be carried at highly subsidised rates. Railway managers complain bitterly that the government expects the Railways to carry this "social cost" without funding them adequately to take over this task.

Indian Railways Aim at Complete Self-seliance

In most developing countries, the running of a modern railway network would not be possible without foreign expertise and importation of rolling stock and other hardware. Not so in India. The Railways are almost entirely self-reliant as far as manufacturing their own equipment is concerned. The first steam locomotive was produced in India in 1873. Today, locomotives are produced in two Railway owned factories while the bulk of the passenger coaches are manufactured in the Integrated Coach Factory in Madras. An additional rail coach factory was set up at Kapurthala in 1988 and will produce 1000 coaches after reaching full capacity. Electrical signaling items, railway tracks and other components are also produced in plants belonging to the Railways.

Export of Railway Technology

The high standard of Indian railway expertise is proven by the fact that India is aiding other developing countries in running or modernizing their own railways. The Integrated Coach Factory, for instance, was able to export bogies and coaches to 11 countries in Asia and Africa against stiff Japanese competition.

Indian Railways, thus, can hold its own both as a cheap means of transport for a population of 860 million and as a modern enterprise which produces industrial goods at a high standard. Inspite of the budgetary constraints under which the Railways are working, they manage to maintain a service which is unique in the developing world. It should not be forgotten that rail transport is also environmentally tolerable—a boon in a world which is chocking from the pollution caused by road traffic.

29

Forest

Global losses of forest area have marched in step with population growth for much of human history. The two trends rose slowly for millennia, turned upward in recent centuries, and accelerated sharply after 1900. Indeed, 75 percent of the historical growth in global population and an estimated 75 percent of the loss in global forested area have occurred in the twentieth century. The correlation makes sense, given the additional need for farmland, pastureland, and forest products as human numbers expand. But since 1950, the advent of mass consumption of forest products has quickened the pace of deforestation.

In some cases, population pressure is still closely linked with deforestation. In Latin America, for example, ranching is the single largest cause of deforestation. Because most meat produced in Latin America is consumed there, and because meat consumption per person has been largely unchanged for several decades, it is likely that expanding population is the principal reason for ranching-related deforestation. In addition, analysts at the World Resources Institute estimate that overgrazing and over collection of firewood-which are often a function of a growing population—are degrading some 14 percent of the world's threatened frontier forests (large areas of virgin fores). In fact, a U.N. Food and Agriculture Organisation study showed a one-to-one correlation between population growth and fuelwood consumption in 16 Asian countries between 1961 and 1994.

On the other hand, deforestation created by the demand for forest products tracks more closely with rising per capita consumption in recent decades, Global use of paper and paperboard per person, for example, has doubled (or nearly tripled) since 1961, and most of the increase has come in wealthy countries with low or even stable levels of population growth. Europe, Japan, and North America, with 16 percent of global population, consume 63 percent of the world's paper and paperboard and nearly half its industrial wood.

Although consumption and population growth have operated somewhat independently in the late twentieth century, the two forces could coincide in the developing world in coming decades, with substantial consequences for forests. Developing-country paper consumption is less than one tenth the level found in industrial nations, suggesting that large increases in consumption are likely as these nations prosper. (It also suggests that greater economy is needed in industrial countries). With 80 percent of the world's people, and as home to all the increase in population in coming decades, even modest growth in per capital paper and wood consumption in developing countries could place substantial pressure on forests. If paper were used by the entire world in 2050 at today's industrial-nation rates, paper production would need to jump more than eightfold over 1996 levels.

This projected growth is unsustainable, given that global use of forest products is already near or beyond the limits of sustainable use. Using data on sustainable forest yields, and assuming that virgin forests are left intact, researchers at Friends of the Earth UK have determined that production of forest products for the world is 25 percent beyond the most restrictive estimates for sustainable consumption. (Many forests, of course, are already logged well beyond sustainable levels). The most optimistic assessment would allow for a further 35-percent growth in consumption. Even that spells trouble, however, given a projected global population increase of some 54 per cent over the next half-century, and given the likely increase in consumption from rising prosperity. Lower consumption of forest products and increased recycling in industrial countries can make room for a more prosperous developing world to enjoy the products of the world's forests, but the task will be made easier if population growth everywhere is stabilized sooner rather than later.

If population and consumption eat into the world's forests, the resulting loss of forest services reduces, in turn, a country's capacity to support its population. Forests provide habitat to a diverse selection of wildlife; tropical forests, for example, are home to more than 50 percent of the world's species. And as storehouses of carbon, forests are key to regulating climate. Deforestation leads to huge releases of carbon: an estimated one quarter of the world's carbon emissions come from forest clearing. Loss of these macroservices undermines the stability and resiliency of the global environment on which economies—and populations—depend. In addition, forests provide services vital to a local population, such as control of erosion, steady provision of water across rainy and dry seasons, and regulation of rainfall. Taken together, the loss of these services due to deforestation can upset local economies and subject local populations to economic instability.

30

Population Growth and Climate Change

Over the last half-century, carbon emissions from fossil fuel burning expanded at nearly twice the rate of population, boosting atmospheric concentrations of carbon dioxide, the principal greenhouse gas, by 30 percent over preindustrial levels. All major scientific bodies acknowledge the likelihood that climate change due to the buildup of greenhouse gases in the atmosphere is indeed under way. The 15 warmest years on record have all occurred since 1979, and 1998.

The destabilization of our climate threatens more intense heat waves, more severe droughts and floods, more destructive storms, and more extensive forest fires. The related shifts in rainfall and temperature may jeopardize food production, the Earth's biological diversity, and entire ecosystems, as well as human health by expanding the ranges of tropical diseases. Unless efforts to curb them are stepped up, carbon emissions will continue to grow faster than population over the next 50 years, driving the Earth's climate system into uncharted territory. The Intergovernmental Panel on Climate Change (IPCC) estimates that an eventual two-thirds reduction in global emissions is needed to avoid precariously high levels of atmospheric carbon dioxide concentrations.

The IPCC and the U.S. Department of Energy (DOE) project that emissions from developing countries will nearly quadruple over the next half-century, while those from industrial nations will increase by 30 percent. Although annual emissions from industrial countries are currently twice as high as from developing ones, the latter are on·target to eclipse the industrial world by 2020.

Higher per capita carbon emissions account for roughly 55 percent of the increase in emissions projected for developing nations. Emissions per person are due to more than double from 0.51 tons of carbon per year in 2000—just one fifth of the industrial level—to 1.14 tons in 2050. The remaining 45 percent of emissions increases is due to population growth.

Fossil fuel use accounts for roughly three quarters of world carbon emissions. As a result, regional growth in carbon emissions tend to occur where economic activity, and related energy use, is projected to growth most rapidly. Emissions in China are projected to grow over three times faster than population in the next half-century, as emissions per person soar from 0.77 tons of carbon to 2.81 tons due to booming economy that is heavily reliant on coal and other carbon-rich energy sources. In Africa, in contrast, emissions per person are expected to scarcely change-growing from the current level of 0.33 tons in 2050, despite a threefold increase in total emissions.

The effects of population growth are most profound in countries where people are heavily emitters. For example, the 115 million people added to the population of the United States between 1950 and 1998-an increase of nearly 75 percent in just 45 years-account for more than one tenth of current global emissions. And the carbon emissions of the 75 million people who will be added to the U.S. population in the next 50 years roughly equal the emissions of the 1.3 billion people who will be added to Africa during that period.

Deforestation and other land use changes account for the remainder of world carbon emissions. Forests have served as a sink for carbon throughout much of human history. In recent years, however, the world's forests have become net sources of atmospheric carbon, largely due to forest burning and clearing in the tropics. Six months of fires in Asia in 1997 and 1998 released more carbon than Western Europe emits from fossil fuel burning in an entire year. The carbon contribution from this source will likely increase in coming years as the burgeoning human population continues to cut down forests.

31
Biodiversity

As human population has surged this century, the populations of numerous other species have tumbled, many to the point of extinction. Indeed, we live amid the greatest extinction of plant and animal life since the dinosaurs disappeared some 65 million years ago, with species losses at 100 to 1,000 times the natural rate. But humans are not just witnesses to a rare historic event, we are actually its cause. The leading sources of today's species loss, habitat alteration, invasions by exotic species, pollution, and overhunting are all a function of human activities.

Human activities have pushed the percentage of mammals, amphibians, land fish that are in "immediate danger" of extinction into double digits. The principal cause of species extinction is habitat loss—the result of encroachment by humans for settlements, for agriculture, or to claim resources such as timber. A particularly productive but vulnerable habitat is found in coastal areas, home to 60 percent of the world's population. Coastal wetlands nurture two thirds of all commercially caught fish, for example. And coral reefs have the second highest concentration of biodiversity in the world, after tropical rainforests. But human encroachment and pollution are degrading these areas: roughly half of the world's salt marshes and mangrove swamps have been eliminated or radically altered, and two thirds of the world's coral reefs have been degraded, 10 percent of them "beyond recognition". As coastal migration continues—coastal dwellers could account for 75 percent of world population within 30 years—the pressures on these productive habitats will likely increase".

Habitat loss tends to accelerate with an increase in a country's population density. This is bad news for the world's biodiversity hotspots-species-rich ecosystems at greatest risk of destruction. Twenty-four of these hotspots, containing half of the planet's species, have been identified globally. Some of the most important hotspot countries will reach population densities that have been linked with very high rates of habitat loss. Five of the six most biologically rich countries could see more than two thirds of their original habitat destroyed by 2050 if this historical relationship holds.

Related to loss of habitat is the growing incidence of plant, animal, insect, and microbial invasions of ecosystems worldwide as human interchange increases. These "exotic species" sometimes dominate local ecosystems, eliminating native species and reducing overall diversity. Exotics are implicated in 68 percent of all fish extinctions in the United States this century, for example. Growth in human travel and commerce explains many accidental invasions by exotics, but foreign species are also deliberately introduced into farms, plantation forests, and aquaculture systems. Although only 1 percent of exotics cause widespread damage, exotic species are the second leading cause, after habitat destruction, of species loss worldwide.

Other, often diffuse effects of expanded human activities also disrupt ecosystems. Nitrogen, for example, is now made available to plants at more than twice the preindustrial rate as a result of fertilizer production, cultivation of nitrogen-fixing crops, and the burning of fossil fuels. This overfertilization of the Earth favours some species at the expense of others, leading to a reduction in diversity and resiliency of land and aquatic ecosystems.

Likewise, greenhouse gas emissions could disrupt ecosystems on a vast scale. As with nitrogen, increased levels of atmospheric carbon may favour some species over others: annuals over perennials, for example, or deciduous trees over evergreens. To the extent that greenhouse gases induce changes in global climate, many species may be at risk as habitats shift or shrink, and as some life forms, such as insects or animals, adapt and migrate more quickly than others, such as plants. And as sea levels rise with a change in climate, ecosystems such as coastal wetlands could be destroyed.

32

The Environment, The Economy and Public Health—An Integrated View

The environment is central to the health of people and their economies. Just as s foetus is totally dependent on the life-support system of the mother during her pregnancy, so the health and vitality of people and their economies are totally dependent on their environments. Unfortunately, many people do not see it that way. They either see the environment as dependent on the economy—such as the politician who says: "let's make the economy strong, then we'll fix the environment when we can afford it"—or they see little connection between health and the environment, whether they are "deep greens" campaigning on ecological issues or doctors treating individual patients and individual illnesses. Whether we are politicians, greens or doctors, is there not a more efficient way to fulfill our aims? For this, a broader perspective is essential.

All economies are sub-systems of the larger environmental system which provides the:

- Sources of energy and materials;
- Sinks for pollution and other wastes;
- Services of water, nutrients and carbon recycling.
- Space for living, working and aesthetics ("a walk in the woods and the song of a bird")

Neglect of this life-support system of the "4 S's" leads to weaker or defunct economies as vegetation, food, soils, water or air become contaminated or exhausted and gradually fail to support economic activity. This is dramatically illustrated in the Aral Sea region, or the collapsed Canadian salmon fishing communities.

Indirect Social Costs

Less catastrophic but still costly is where economic damage is caused by pesticides and nutrient contamination of groundwater, involving millions of Rupees in water treatment. This is a social cost to the economy that the agricultural sector does not include in the price of its food: an economic distortion that reduces the real wealth of society via false price signals that encourage the over-use of pesticides and fertilisers. Similarly, the "external" costs on society of road-respiratory-induced accidents, noise, respiratory and circulatory diseases and congestion amount to a lot of money to any government but these costs are not borne by transport uses, which mean that transport is encouraged beyond the level that is economic for society as a whole. By internalising these externalities via taxes and other means, the market prices for transport would become fairer and more efficient. Currently only about 30% of transport externalities are covered by transport taxes. But if the health of an economy is dependent on the health of its environment, what about the health of its people?

Without access to the basics of clean water, shelter, fresh air and food, people obviously suffer. Even in more developed economies where the link between everyday life and the environment is not so visible, the role of environmental factors in disease and well-being is significant. Most of the major diseases such as heart disease, cancer, respiratory diseases and allergies have an environmental as well as a genetic component within a multi-factorial chain of causation. And while each environmental factor may be small, if the links in the chain of causation are inter-dependent, as they often appear to be then removing even a small link can break the chain.

Environment Factors

Take asthma in children, for example. There seem to be many causes, from a child's genetic inheritance to its nutritional status, which in tum help determine how it reacts to the many environmental factors, both indoor (such as mites, pets, damp, environmental tobacco smoke, nitrogen oxides) and outdoor (such as pollen and pollution from industry and traffic), that have been implicated in asthma causation. Therefore it is clear that diagnoses of asthma and many other diseases should systematically embrace environmental factors. This will be a significant challenge for doctors whose time is scarce and whose training is not usually appropriate.

This multi-causal chain will vary in its exact make-up from child to child, but for children overall, even if the environmental factors such as damp housing or traffic fumes may be less important than, say, genetic make-up or nutritional status, the environmental factors may be the ones that can be most cost effectively removed, thus breaking the casual chain. And, as with many environmental issues, there are secondary benefits of action, such as less noise or fewer accidents from traffic reduction, or energy savings from dry houses, which further justify the environmental actions even where exact causations are not well understood.

The environmental causes of disease and ill health are a controversial and ill understood area of science and opinions vary about their significance. Some say that, for Western Europe, perhaps 2-3% of public disease and ill-health is determined by known environmental factors but others maintain that it must be far more significant. They point to the sharp increase over the last two or three decades in asthma, allergies, and cancers (particularly of the reproductive organs such as breast and testicles) and related ill-health such as sperm count decline, which cannot be explained by genetic causes. They also observe that the large differences in health between the socio-economic classes cannot be explained without involving significant environmental causation.

It is thought that the ubiquitous presence of low doses of mixtures of chemicals in food, drink, air, consumer products and the general environment are playing some role in public ill health, even if the evidence for this is afar from substantial.

Impact on Public Health

But what about environmental programmes and campaigns being little concerned with health? Well, history so far shows that the environment only gets serious attention when it is seen to be damaging either the economy or public health. Yet because "everything connects" in "socio—enviro" systems, action to stop infectious diseases from water contamination, or to reduce skin cancer from ozone depletion, leads to a better environment for all species. And if upland forests are preserved because they are seen to be cheaper and more effective water regulators (which reduce the risk of lowland flooding) than dams, then upland biodiversity benefits anyway, even if it was last in the queue for political attention.

Although public health may be seen by some as only a small part of "the environment", much environmental progress depends upon the political weight of the health impacts. For example, the cost benefit exercise on the current multi-pollutant/effect programme on acidification, eutrophication and low-level ozone shows that it is the benefits to human health, not eco-system damage, that provide the main economic justification for further reductions in SO_2, NO_x and NH_3. Ecologists need the language of public health in order to maximise political support for the environment. So, it is out of our specialist "boxes" of economics, health and ecology, and into a shared systems approach, with integrated programmes that build partnerships for progress.

33

Measuring Population's Impact

There is no easy way to measure the overall impact of human activities on the environment. Nevertheless, several approaches have been developed as follows:

Environmental Resource Accounting

Environmental resource accounting attempts to place an economic value on "environmental goods and services" used –natural resources that conventionally have been regarded as free and used in common. These include unpolluted freshwater clean air, ocean life, forests, and wetlands.

Some economists argue that the value of environmental goods and services should be incorporated into estimates of Gross manufactured capital, which depreciates in value overtime, environmental capital (such as forests, fisheries, and unpolluted air and water) currently is not considered to depreciate, and no charge is made against current income as it is used. A country could exhaust its mineral resources, cut down its forests, erode its soils, pollute its acquires, and hunt its wildlife and fisheries to extinction, but measured income would not be affected as these natural assets disappeared.

If natural resources were valued in the same way that manufactured assets are valued, it might help economies learn to use them more efficiently and to conserve them in order to assure continued use in the future. Such valuations also might help indicate the economic benefits of protecting the environment, as well as the ecological benefits. In other terms, instead of continuing to draw down their "environmental capital" until it is gone, economies could begin to live on its interest, maintaining the capital for use indefinitely in the future.

I = P x A x T

The equation I=PxAxT represents another effort to describe the overall impact of humanity on the environment. In the equation:

- **I** is environmental impact
- **P** is population (including size, growth, and distribution)
- **A** is the level of affluence (consumption per capita), and
- **T** is the level of technology.

Despite its limitations—for instance, inability to assign actual values to each component or to depict changes in the factors over time—the equation is valuable. In particular, it emphasizes that developing countries with large and rapidly growing populations affect the environment, even though their levels of affluence may be low, while at the same time countries in the developed world with little or no population growth have a substantial environmental impact because consumption per capita is so high.

The equation makes clear that slowing population growth is a key part of any strategy to reduce humanity's impact on the environment. For example, even if per capita resource consumption (A) declined or technologies (T) improved enough to reduce the environmental impact (I) of humanity by 10%, this gain would be wiped out in less than a decade because world population (P) is growing at over 1% per year since per capital consumption of resources is expected to increase as living standards, rise, protecting the environment requires more efficient production technologies, less waste, and ultimately a stable world population size.

Ecological Footprints of Nations

Every body has an impact on the Earth, because they consume the products and services of nature. Their ecological impact corresponds to the amount of nature they occupy to keep them going. In other words, we calculate the 'ecological footprints' of these countries.

Carrying Capacity

The term "carrying capacity" refers to the number of people the earth can support. Logically, population growth must stop at some point, or the earth would become overcrowded and its resources eventually would be depleted. But what is this maximum human population?

This question has been debated since 1798, when English economists Thomas Malhus predicted that population growth inevitably would outstrip the food and water supply at some point. Since the estimates of carrying capacity have varied a great deal depending on what assumptions are made out technology, consumption, levels, and other factors that are not easily forecast. Some have even argued that the earth's carrying capacity may already have been exceeded in sense that the world consumed at the rate that Americans and Western European consume

While no body can know how many people the earth could support, few would want to find out the hard way—by reaching this theoretical limit. Calculate the maximum number of people who could exist on earth seems less important than determining how resources can be used wisely and managed sustainably to improve living standard without eventually destroying the natural environment that supports life itself.

34

What was Wrong with Structural Adjustment

In Defence of a Much-Maligned Strategy

After decades of stranded development theories, ideologies and paradigms, "structural adjustment", with its demands for clean fiscal policy and an end to uneconomic state enterprises, political privileges, market and exchange rate intervention and corruption, entered the aid arena like a refreshing dawn after a long night of frustrating dreams. Only the "old guard" of planned economy advocated and jealous academicians who had missed the boat were able to shut their eyes to the moral and economic justification of this liberating break-through in international development policy spearheaded by the Breton Woods institutions then steered by some exceptionally courageous economists.

Reaction to Saps

As with any revolution, defeat is awaiting the pioneers at the hands of political power greed, reactionary tactics by the formerly privileged and academic envy. The principal device serving the reactionary forces as a lever of influence on the mood of the "development community" has been the identification and dramatisation of new pockets or strata of (principally urban) poverty allegedly created by structural adjustment measures, while shunning the much broader-based rise in economic activity, real incomes and sense of fair reward in the overall society, especially the rural population. That the hardship experienced by urban poor, formerly privileged under consumer price control and import subsidies to the debit of depressed farm prices or maintained by grossly over-expanded public payrolls, was only laying open the camouflaged erosion of the economy and near-bankruptcy of governments and public enterprises was conveniently downplayed.

These reactionary howls were to be expected. Not that they met the entirely innocent. There had been naively sweeping, overly assuming demands by some structural adjustment missions. But an intellectually vigorous and dynamic "development community" would have coped with the ensuing opposition, strengthened the analytical and monitoring capacities and the political will to endure also rocky roads and bitter medicines on the way to a healthier base. Instead, institutional rivalry, political opportunism and emotive populism were thriving. In a way, the "development community" behaved as if it did not want its patient to become able to stand on his own feet and eventually steal its raison d'être.

Worst, the Bretton Woods institutions themselves, partly under the pressure of the emotive opposition described above fell to the temptation to rescue their lending volume, which was threatened by the frugality dictated to third World public budgets under structural adjustment recipes, through hardship-easing loans. They thereby corrupted their creation in suing it to reinforce their indispensability. As a consequence it soon turned out that some of the most obedient loan takers under structural adjustment terms experienced sharply rising indebtedness, exploited as a disqualifying symptom by the anti-structural adjustment camp.

Whatever the opinions on structural adjustment policies, the commitment to the principles of "good governance" has come to stay, at least on paper, as an almost standard conditionally for official development aid from OECD donor countries. The realisation, matured in the implementation of structural adjustment programmes, that not the quantity of aid, but the quality of Third World governments determines the positive or negative course of development, may be regarded as the most valuable fruit of the decades-old-policy debate in the "development community". And the use of aid as a pressure or bribing factor towards "good governance" as foreign aid's least disputable purpose.

Out of the Limelight

Nothing, however, must be taken for granted. Achievement breeds its challenge! Structural adjustment, though in essence hardly disputable has been pushed out of the limelight and replaced by the oldest actor in the company: eradication of poverty, twinned with an equally perpetual endeavour at the macro-level: debt-forgiveness. This falling back to square one in donors' approach to the problems of the south, i.e., the call to alleviate poverty and priorities direct efforts to this end above all other developmental efforts—does it indicate a sell-out of constructive ideas in the 'development community'? Has any noteworthy progress been achieved in the past by this approach?

By telling a frugally toiling but independent subsistence farmer that internationally his condition is classed as "poverty", deserving compassion and support by the world community and cancellation of his debts, one can hardly expect a sustainable improvement in his output, satisfaction, or self-respect and even less, when he realises that the help principally provides jobs, fringe benefits and self-importance to a gamut of intermediaries, at home and abroad.

What do those poverty advocates (the "Lords of poverty") really know about the resources, life management, value systems and ambitions of those they generalise by the billions? The great variance in the conception of life situations, from different external viewpoints.

What the aid system can do for these rural populations classed as "poor"/ "underprivileged"/ "exploited", is press for justice, i.e., "good governance". The achievements of structural adjustment policy through e.g., abolishing official price and exchange rate distortions, import subsidies and exploitative state agencies, has brought massive income improvement for peasant populations, i.e., the majority of LDC inhabitants, in dimensions unreachable by whatsoever direct "attack" on rural "poverty". What people want is not being benevolently treated as poor, but being justly rewarded for their work, i.e., by access to the unmanipulated market value of their output. Slackening on structural adjustment/ "good governance" conditionally under the present "10 year itch" for paradigm change means foregoing much of the potential opportunities for undoing injustice and exploitation of the masses. It should be clear where priority focus should be placed in ODA policy.

Small Is Not Beautiful

The direct attack on "poverty", orchestrated by the Bretton Woods institutions under their freshly launched Poverty Reduction Strategy Paper (PRSP) campaign, is being rightly regarded as primarily an NGO domain, since most activities are expected to be carried out at local community level. This would require careful screening and coordinating of NGO activities and their integration via gradual expansion of their experience. But "small" is not "beautiful" for the development financing institutions. Disbursement needs are pressing, calling for the new paradigm to quickly provide channels for another wave of loans to the "IDA Countries". Their problem of heavy indebtedness, which would principally exclude most of them from any new loan consideration, shall be solved with one stroke (which only the well-cushioned development bureaucracy can afford); debt relief against presentation of country PRSPs by the respective governments. NGOs are expected to play in the system especially the knowledge gap about the "poor" people's real wants and needs NGOs will naturally be tempted by such expansionary boost to their involvement (referred to sarcastically as their philanthropic empire" by an African conference participant), but this will not be conducive to quality and accountability of their performance, which ideally should be based on private sponsorship in combination with strong target-group provided self-help components.

Patience and Self-Restraint

Local knowledge and initiatives cannot be obtained under time pressure. "The grass does not grow faster by being pulled". When will the "development community" learn patience and self-restraint in the approach to LDC's capacity for constructive absorption of aid programmes accompanied by a genuine sense of ownership?

After all these deliberations, how shall development policy be shaped in order to better correspond with reality, without sinking deeper into hypocrisy and frustration?

To come back to the opening question: what was wrong with "structural adjustment"? Nothing was wrong with its intent. In fact this was very right and long overdue. Its implementation, however, lacked patience, perseverance and solid support from the development community, apart from its being corrupted as a vehicle for expansionary lending policy. If aid is meant to not be an end in itself, then structural adjustment policy needs constant reinforcement, underpinned by strict lending discipline. There should be an end to irresponsible lending and easy escape from its consequences by wholesome periodic debt relief burdened on the international tax-paying community. No ODA, either loans or grants, should be made available to governments who are not in active process of implementing "good governance" principles. A monitoring unit, reporting to the donor community on government performance in regard to its "good government"? Structural adjustment commitment, should be maintained in each and receiving country by "donor consortia" comprising all locally represented bilateral and multilateral development organisations currently extending technical, financial or material assistance to the country.

In order to accommodate the poverty focus without diluting the necessary structural adjustment orientation of ODA, a division of activity-focus between the latter and the NGO sector would seem to be advantageous.

- ODA, limited to the countries abiding to structural adjustment/ "good governance" conditionally, with focus concentration on sustainable physical, social and economic infrastructure principally at national and regional level, public management training, higher education and research, consultant and senior adviser services.

- the NGO sector, principally funded by private sponsorship, united to structural adjustment conditionally (but preferably grafted on local self-help initiative), with focus-concentration on the third World "poor", i.e., mostly at rural community and low-income township level, for amelioration of living conditions and local resource utilisation.
- strengthening of linkages between the NGO sector and the UN Technical Agencies to mutual benefit: NGOs in need of professional information, evaluation and advice or forum for discussion to find an actively supportive window at the agencies; the latter to maintain and develop field contact for research and policy generation, not least as a substitute for their declining project work (giving way to greater concentration on their global functions i.e., serving as information, policy initiation, and coordination/negotiation center on topics of global concern, such as e.g.: human rights, global monetary and trade systems, tropical forest and global marine resources, global and Regional health threats, international standards.)

In conclusion, it may be called to mind that aid and its institutions have no claim for permanence. They are justified only as temporary functions in a phasing-out process of self-help support. Any claim for unlimited continuity would breed lasting infantilisation.

35

Ecosystems, our Unknown Protectors

How ecosystems work and what part they play in biodiversity remain a mystery. But we do know that they perform a host of invaluable services for the human species. In my view, biodiversity's fundamental value is neither aesthetic nor economic but environmental, even though most people are largely unaware of this. The value of biodiversity is often measured in terms of the number of species living in a given area. But the interactions between the many species in an ecosystem, and between them and the environment's physical and chemical components are also very important. This highly intricate web of relationships makes an ecosystem more valuable than the sum of the species it contains.

Ecosystems perform services that are essential for the survival of the human species. They fix carbon in the atmosphere and produce oxygen, protect soil from erosion and keep it fertile, filter water and replenish aquifers, provide pollination and anti-parasite agents and so on.

The first two of these services are closely related to each other. They result from photosynthesis, whereby green plants, starting with algae, absorb carbon dioxide (CO_2) and emit oxygen. For millions of years, the balance between the various gases in the atmosphere remained stable. But with the coming of the industrial revolution, humans began burning increase amounts of fossil fuels. Today, three billion tonnes of carbon build up in the atmosphere each year, and natural ecosystems can no longer absorb all these emissions—especially since they are disappearing at an alarming rate.

Deforestation alone releases such tremendous amounts of CO_2 and other gases, such as methane, that it has become the second-leading cause of global warming.

Storing freshwater, protecting soil and keeping it fertile are three other closely related functions. Ecosystems are veritable "freshwater factories". They absorb rainwater and slowly filter it through the soil before draining it towards streams, rivers, lakes and underground aquifers that supply us with the precious liquid. When the vegetal ground cover is degraded, the water cycle is disrupted. Rain strikes the bare earth, washing away huge amounts of nutritional substances. Reservoirs, lakes and rives silt up.

Uncertain Reaction to Climate Change

Despite years of research, scientists still know very little about how ecosystems work. We are generally incapable of predicting how they will react to certain transformations in the environment, especially climate changes. Nor do we know any more about whether a species present in a given environment is superfluous or "replicable", even when it is very rare. Likewise, we do not know which key species are indispensable to maintaining an ecosystem, with a few exceptions such as pine forests, where that tree is obviously the dominant species.

We know even less about the part biological diversity itself play in maintaining ecosystems and the services they perform. One simple example is a highest diversified forest that absorbs carbon dioxide—a vital function, as we have seen, for limiting global warming. Suppose the forest is cleared to make way for a single-crop forest. The service will still be performed, perhaps even better at first because young, fast-growing trees absorb more CO_2 than old ones, which regenerate slowly. But what will happen in the long term? After several decades, the consequences of the loss of biodiversity will probably be felt. Replacing many species with a single one will have certainly depleted the soil and, in the long term, slowed down the forest's growth and consequently its ability to absorb CO_2.

More generally, diversified ecosystems seem more productive. Specialists remain wary about their conclusions, but today they believe that biodiversity helps ecosystems to resist alien species and diseases and to recover faster in the event of disruption. In the face of doubt, and to find out more about them, it is better to preserve as many different ecosystems as possible.

A Costly Lesson for New York City

Most people take it for granted that ecosystems will carry on performing services without receiving anything in return. They think nature will continue benefiting humanity, no matter how much damage is done. The survival of organisms other than our own species is perceived as a frill that future generations can live without.

These preconceived ideas are wrong and dangerous, as the city of New York has recently come to realize. The city's water has always enjoyed such a good reputation that it was sold throughout the northeastern United States. Its equality was due to Catskill Mountains' natural purification system. But that ecosystem has suffered so much from pollution, especially fertilizer run-off from farms, that by the late 1990s New York's water had become undrinkable. The city planned to build a purification plant, whose cost was put at between six and eight billion dollars, not including the $300 million in yearly operating costs—an astronomical bill for a service that had always been free! The price was so staggering that the city eventually decided to restore the Catskill Mountains' degraded environment at a cost of only one billion dollars.

This story clearly illustrates where our interests lie. We must preserve ecosystems and the conditions that enable our planet to ensure the survival of *Homo sapiens* or, at least, the short-term maintenance of our current quality of life.

36

Finance Matters—Financial Liberalisation: Too Much too Soon?

An efficient and stable financial system is important for economic growth and poverty reduction. The financial crises that have afflicted many countries in recent times have been a costly and painful reminder of the disastrous consequences for development of weak financial markets. The recurrence of financial crises, at both the international and national levels, and the adverse effect they have had on economic growth and poverty levels, have highlighted the need for a policy framework which addresses the inherent vulnerability of financial markets to systemic instability and failure.

Governments have always intervened in the financial sector and there are sound theoretical and practical reasons for doing so. Financial markets are characterised by problems of limited and unequal information, making them inherently imperfect and prone to failure. Financial regulation and supervision are therefore essential for efficient and stable financial market development. How should governments intervene? Have financial liberalisation and financial sector reform made financial systems more, or less vulnerable to instability and systemic crises? How can the process be better managed? What is the best policy framework for supporting financial sector development in low-income countries.

Repression to Liberalisation

For many years, governments followed a policy of financial 'repression', which relied on fixing interest rates below market levels and controlling the allocation of credit. The economic distortions induced by these policies were considerable. Financial systems remained underdeveloped, lending patterns were inefficient and failed to achieve their distributional goals. Negative real interest rates led to low savings and encouraged capital flight. Macro-economic performance also deteriorated countries with large negative real interest rates experienced lower allocation efficiency and growth rates. In the state owned banking sector, poor lending decisions (often politically influenced) and low repayment rates led to bank insolvency and large budgetary bailouts of depositors and creditors.

A growing awareness of the economic costs of financial 'repression', led to financial 'liberalisation' as the dominant policy paradigm over the past two decades. Initially, the relaxation of controls on interest rates was the focus for financial reform which was often triggered by a financial crisis. The relaxation of controls on the financial sector was often part of a more general policy shift towards liberalisation of the domestic economy and opening upto the international economy liberalisation soon broadened therefore beyond interest rate liberalisation, to include a wide range of measures constituting a programme of financial sector reform was adopted under World Bank sectoral or structural adjustment lending conditionalities, the key elements of which included privatisation of banks, entry of new domestic and foreign entrants into the banking sector, bank restructuring and recapitalisation, opening upto the capital account, strengthening bank regulation and supervision institutions.

Has Financial Liberalisation Worked

The period of financial liberalisation coincided with, or was soon followed by heightened financial instability, culminating in the dramatic financial crisis in East Asia in the second half of the 1990s. Clearly, financial liberalisation has not led to a smooth transition to a stable and efficient financial system. It would be wrong, however, to jump to the easy, but shallow, conclusion that financial liberalisation has 'failed'. Firstly, the fact that the period of increased systemic instability does not prove causality. Secondly, no process of change comes cheap: a reasoned assessment of the costs and benefits of the policy change is needed. And thirdly, what would have been the outcome without the policy change". Finally the impact of financial liberalisation will differ between countries, depending on each country's economic and institutional characteristics. The more relevant research issue, therefore, relates to the design and timing of context-specific policy measures, which will contribute to the development of an efficient and stable financial system. Could financial liberalisation have been managed better? If so, what policies are now needed? The commercial banks are the dominant component of the financial sector in low-income countries and are critical to the efficiency and stability of the financial system as a whole. Financial liberalisation was associated with a shift in prudential regulation from direct regulation of banks, by for example, regular site visits, to an indirect approach based on the monitoring of bank capital to ensure that it remained adequate in relation to the risk being taken. Additional regulatory measures are also necessary to restrain the activities of the privatised and other newly-established private banks. The regulatory and supervisory framework may also need to be extended, to cover microfinance institutions which have developed significant deposit taking capacity.

Four main obstacles to efficient banking regulations are:

(a) information, contracting and monitoring problems,

(b) lack of supervisory personnel,

(c) high operational costs and

(d) poor credibility and regulation of regulatory bodies. The appropriateness of various policy measures for dealing with these constraints are discussed and ranked in terms of their suitability for low-income countries. What are the implications of allowing microfinance institutions to offer a range of financing services beyond small-scale lending.

Too Much, too Soon?

The experience with financial liberalisation reveals a strong correlation between liberalisation and financial crisis. This can be explained partly by the exposure of existing inefficiencies and distortions in the financial structure, and partly by a failure to develop a strong regulatory and supervisory framework, prior to liberalisation. Weakness in the initial conditions affect the ability of the privatised banks and new market entrants, to operate on broadly commercial principles. Borrowers are often unable to service their loans, due to poor quality lending and high interest rates. Liberalisation of the capital account increases the inflow of foreign capital, but at the same time threatens that stability of the financial institutions by increasing the exchange rate and domestic lending risks.

The existing regulatory and supervisory system may be unsuited to a market-based environment. Consequently, across-the-board 'big-bang' financial liberalisation and financial sector reform increase the likelihood of systemic crisis, where the institutional and human resource environment is weak. Much of the blame for post-liberalisation financial crisis lies, therefore, with the scale and sequencing of financial reform. What is needed is a more gradual and considered approach to financial liberalisation, which recognises that institutional strengthening, especially in the regulation and supervision capacity, is a prerequisite for creating a more efficient and stable financial sector which can contribute fully to achieving economic growth and poverty reduction in developing countries.

Bibliography

De Soto, H., 1990. *The Other Path: The Invisible Revolution in the Third World.* Reprint edition. New York: Harper Collins.

Doha Development Agenda, 2001. The Ministerial Declaration and other Decisions and Declarations from the Doha Ministerial Conference. Available: http://www.wto.org/english/tratop_e/dda_e/dda_e.htm.

English, P., B. Hoekman, and A. Mattoo, 2002. *Development, Trade and the WTO: A Handbook.* The World Bank, Washington D.C.

Feketekuty, G., 1988. *International Trade in Services: An Overview and Blueprint for Negotiations.* Cambridge, MA: American Enterprise Institute/Ballinger.

Finger, J.M., 1993. *Antidumping: How It Works and Who Gets Hurt.* Ann Arbor: Univ. of Michigan Press.

——, 2001. "Implementing the Uruguay Round Agreements: Problems for Developing Countries." *The World Economy* 24 (9, September): 1097-108.

Finger, J.M. and J.J. Nogues, 2001. The Unbalanced Uruguay Round Outcome: The New Areas in Future WTO Negotiations. Policy Research Working Paper No. 2732, The World Bank, Washington, D.C.

Finger, J.M. and L. Schuknecht, 2001. "Market Access Advances and Retreats: The Uruguay Round and Beyond." In B. Hoekman and W. Martin, eds., *Developing Countries and the WTO: A Pro-active Agenda.* Oxford: UK and Malden. Also available as Policy Research Working Paper No. 2232 at http://www.worldbank.org/research/trade.

Finger, J.M. and P. Schuler, 2000. "Implementation of Uruguay Round Commitments: The Development Challenge." *The World Economy* 23 (4, April): 511-25. Also available as Policy Research Working Paper No. 2215 at http://www.worldbank.org/research/trade.

Finger, J.M. and L.A. Winters, 2002. "Reciprocity." In P. English, B. Hoekman, and A. Mattoo, *Development, Trade and the WTO: A Handbook.* The World Bank, Washington D.C.

Finger, J.M., M.D. Ingco, and U. Reincke, 1996. *The Uruguay Round: Statistics on Tariff Concessions given and Received.* The World Bank, Washington, D.C.

Finger, J.M., F. Ng, and S. Wangchuk, 2001. Antidumping as Safeguard Policy. Policy Research Working Paper No. 2730, The World Bank, Washington, D.C.

Francois, J.F., B. McDonald, and H. Nordstrom, 1996. "The Uruguay Round: A Numerically Based Qualitative Assessment." In W. Martin and L.A. Winters, eds., *The Uruguay Round and the Developing Countries.* Cambridge: Cambridge University Press.

Harrison, G.W., T.F. Rutherford, and D.G. Tarr, 1996. "Quantifying the Uruguay Round." In W. Martin and L.A. Winters, eds., *The Uruguay Round and the Developing Countries.* Cambridge: Cambridge University Press.

Hudec, R.E., 1970. "The GATT Legal System: A Diplomat's Jurisprudence." *Journal of World Trade Law* 4:615-65.

International Intellectual Property Alliance (IIPA), 2002a. "Description of the IIPA." Available: http://www.iipa.com/aboutiipa.html.

——, 2002b. "Statistics." Available: http://www.iipa.com/statistics.html.

Martin, W. and L.A. Winters, 1996. *The Uruguay Round and the Developing Countries.* Cambridge: Cambridge University Press.

Martin, W. and L.A. Winters, 1996. "The Uruguay Round: A milestone for the Developing Countries." in W. Martin and L.A. Winters, eds., *The Uruguay Round and the Developing Countries.* Cambridge: Cambridge University Press.

Maskus, K.E., 2000. *Intellectual Property Rights in the Global Economy.* Institute for International Economics, Washington, D.C.

Michalopulos, C., 1999. "The Developing Countries in the WTO." *The World Economy* 22 (1) January.

O'Neill, T. and G. Hymel (contributor), 1995. *All Politics Is Local: And Other Rules of the Game.* Reprint edition. Massachusetts: Adams Media Corporation.

Panagariya, A., forthcoming. "Developing Countries at Doha: A Political Economy Analysis". *The World Economy.*

Petersen, M. and D.G. McNeil Jr., 2001. "Maker Yielding Patent in Africa for AIDS Drug" *The New York Times.* 15 March. Page 1.

Preeg, E.H., 1995. *Traders in a Brave New World.* Chicago and London: University of Chicago Press.

Reichman, J.H., 1998. "Securing Compliance with the TRIPS Agreement after US v India." *Journal of International Economic Law* 1(4, December): 603-06.

Ricupero, R., 2000. "A Development Round: Converting Rhetoric Into Substance." Paper presented at the Symposium on Efficiency, Equity and Legitimacy: The Multilateral Trading System at the Millennium, 1-2 June, John F. Kennedy School of Government, Harvard University, Cambridge, Massachusetts.

Shaffer, G., 2002. "The law-in Action of International Trade Litigation: The Blurring of the Public and the Private." University of Wisconsin Law School, Madison. Manuscript.

Winham, G., 1986. *International Trade and The Tokyo Round of Negotiations.* Princeton: Princeton University Press.

Winters, L.A., 2002. "Doha and the World Poverty Targets." Paper prepared for the Annual Bank Conference on Development Economics (ABCDE), 29-30 April, World Bank, Washington, D.C.

World Bank, 2002. *Global Economic Prospects and the Developing Countries.* The World Bank, Washington D.C.

World Trade Organization (WTO), 2002a. "WTO Secretariat Budget for 2002." Available: http://www.wto.org/english/thewto_e/secre_e/budget_e.htm.

——, 2002b. Pledging Conference to provide sound financial basis for Doha Agenda. Available: http://www.wto.org/english/news_e/press02_e/pr277_e.htm.

Zeller, T.W., 1992. *America Trade and Power in the 1960s.* New York: Columbia.

Index